THE
DEACON

Meet the
Author

Ada E. Crain was born in 1904 in Goltry, a town in the Cherokee Strip, Indian Territory, now in the State of Oklahoma. Her father and grandfather's family had traveled from Angola, Indiana, to Kansas by wagon train in 1878.

Ada's high school years were spent in Republic, Missouri. She received a B.S. Degree in Education from Southwest Missouri University in 1928 with her first teaching position at Brandsville High School in Missouri.

Moving to Michigan in 1930, she taught in Atlanta for 12 years, followed by a year in Harbor Beach, a year in Blissfield, and 12 years in Big Rapids. She served as Principal in both Atlanta and Blissfield, Michigan.

Arriving in Fowlerville, Michigan in 1957, Ada served as High School Librarian for 12 years, and Fowlerville Public Librarian until 1965. During her teaching years she also studied at the University of Missouri, the National University of Mexico, and Michigan State University, earning her Master's Degree.

She has traveled widely through 16 countries as well as 34 states in the U.S.A. She has also been listed in both *The World Who's Who of Women* and *2000 Women of Achievment*.

THE DEACON

ADA E. CRAIN

Copyright © 1994 by Ada E. Crain

Library of Congress Catalog Card Number: 94-93912

ISBN: 0-9643286-0-7

Typesetting by:

Red Cedar PrintShop
1824 Maple Shade Dr.
Williamston, MI 48895

Published by Ada E. Crain

DEDICATION

This book is dedicated to
the memory of
my parents
Ernest and Maudie Owens Crain

ACKNOWLEDGEMENTS

I would like to acknowledge the people who helped me with this book.

My special thanks goes to Yvonne Hasty for her constant inspiration and encouragement while I was writing this book, and also for her proof-reading of the manuscript.

My thanks also to Clayton and Marjorie Klein for editing, preparation of the map, and for proof-reading my manuscript.

TABLE OF CONTENTS

INTRODUCTION

The Deacon, who was my father, was an outstanding pioneer.

As I sit here thinking about the story of my father's long life, I have a picture in my mind of an old man, perhaps seventy years of age, sitting on an old bench under a huge black walnut tree, talking to himself about the events of the day. The bench he is sitting on isn't an ordinary bench. It was a pew taken from the old Congregational Church of Republic, Missouri in about 1930. Nor is the elderly man an ordinary man. He is about five feet eight inches tall with gray, almost white hair, a dark brown mustache and piercing blue eyes. He weighs about 180 pounds and is dressed in a blue chambray shirt and blue pants held up by old–fashioned suspenders. He always said he couldn't wear a belt.

His clothes are wet with sweat from working in his vegetable garden. He is talking to himself as was his habit from living alone on an Oklahoma homestead for so many years.

He always parted his hair on one side and let it grow long because the top of his head was bald. My mother and I used to tell him that he "was stealing" but he didn't seem to mind our teasing.

If one listened carefully, one could tell what his thoughts were without having to ask.

The family pet, a big tiger tomcat, has followed him from the garden and is sitting on its tail on the sidewalk listening and seeming to understand every word that is said.

My father was a man of the "old school", wise, stern, dominant, honest and cranky but always trying to lead his little girl in what to him was the right way. His was an unusual but interesting existence.

Early in life I conceived the idea of writing a book about his life but many facts I did not know as he seldom talked about his family. He was a silent man and had some family experiences that were distasteful to him and this molded his character into the sort of being that he became.

I chose the Allen County Library in Fort Wayne, Indiana as my first place to write for records. I was fortunate to receive a complete record of the cemeteries, marriages, deaths, and land transactions as well as the 1885 history of Steuben County, Indiana.

I had very little to help me when I began to research father's family. He always said that the family name of Crain was an old English spelling and that the family came from Wales to Canada then to Steuben County, Indiana. He told me his father's name was Orange, named after William of Orange who ruled England for several years and that his mother's name was Delilah. His grandfather was named Ezekiel and that was all I had to go on.

So my warning to all teenagers is that you may grow tired of your parents' stories regarding their lives but there may come a time when you will wish you could remember some of those things. Sometimes it may make a difference in your life or your family's lives as to how much you can remember.

Memory is a queer thing. It may leave you when you need it most. You may resent and dislike hearing the old stories but my advice is to copy facts as you hear them and don't be afraid to ask questions. You will be glad you did, when you are older and there is no one left to help you.

I can remember hearing many of my friends and relatives say, "I can't help you". If I had just copied down facts when I was young, I would be so relieved and have something more to work on.

Now, as I go back to this story, about all I had to work with was that I had heard my father say that he was born in Steuben County, Indiana, and that the family lived in a little place called Pleasant Lake. I may have to mix a little imagination with the facts to bring out the stories of his life and character.

VERMONT

In the next few paragraphs I shall be quoting from The History of Steuben County 1885, Pleasant Township pages 647–694 for both my great–grandfather and great–grandmother.

Ezekiel Crain was born in Orange County, Vermont, and in 1823 was married to Rebecca Demary (French Canadian) who was born in lower Canada presumably close to what is now Hamilton, Ontario. So far, I have found nothing more about her earlier life as I have not researched in Canada. The family immigrated by ox team to Washtenaw County, Michigan in 1835.

It was in Washtenaw County that their youngest child, Elizabeth, was born. My middle name, Elizabeth, comes from that ancestor. The family lived near Ann Arbor, Michigan not quite three years and then came to Steuben County, Angola, Indiana in 1838. Ezekiel's reasons for coming to Michigan from Canada are not known to me.

I have tried to trace the name Ezekiel Crain back to Orange County, Vermont but have been unsuccessful. My father said this family originally came from Wales. Beyond that, I have no further knowledge. I would guess that the New World and its richness brought relief from poverty, a new religious outlook, a feeling of adventure and hope for a new life.

I joined the Vermont Genealogical Society and hired a man to trace the records in Montpelier but it is difficult to trace records made in the late 1700's. They are almost non–existent. We did find an Elijah Crain in the Second Census Record of the United States in 1800 who had five children under ten years old. Whether one of the children was Ezekiel or not I do not know. We also found that this Elijah was married twice, a property owner, and committed suicide.

My Vermont researcher also sent me a genealogy of the Crane Family, Vol. II in which the name Orange is mentioned frequently in New Jersey records. Also mentioned were the names Gamaliel and Ezekiel. My father said the name Orange was for William of Orange who become the ruler of England and was admired by the Cranes (Craines). This had something to do with their migration from Wales. Whether they came for political reasons or economic reasons is not known, but the name Orange had something to do with it. Several other states have the name Orange as counties and towns.

According to my father, our family always spelled our name Crain because it was the old English spelling. However, I have found both spellings in the same family.

INDIANA

Ezekiel and Rebecca Crain came by ox team to Steuben County, Pleasant Lake, Indiana, in 1835. Here they bought and settled their family on a farm where they built a log cabin that was their home until they died; he in 1863 and Rebecca in 1879. Eight children were born to them one of whom died at birth. The other six sons and one daughter grew up, married, and had families. Of the seven children, five were born in Canada, one in Michigan, and one in Steuben County. The children, in order of their birth, A.D. or Abram, Orange, Nicholas, Richard, Benjamin, Elizabeth, and Chester.

A.D. (Abram) was twelve years old when he arrived in Indiana and assisted his father and his country. He had ten children, all of whom were pioneers, teachers, doctors, or musicians, highly respected in the community.

The second child, Orange, was my grandfather. Orange married Delilah Stealey or Staley. Delilah Staley's father was Elder Staley who came to Pleasant Lake from Marion County, Ohio. He was Pennsylvania Dutch, a Free Will Baptist minister who bought the first land in Pleasant Township, established the first school in one of the rooms of his house, performed the first marriage ceremony in the township, and was father to Lydia, the first white child born in the township. Delilah was one of his younger children.

I have written for information on the Staley's reasons for coming to Indiana but had the door closed in my face. I was told that information was not to be given out. Why, I don't know. That can be the way of genealogy research. In Steuben County the family was highly respected and did many good things.

Now, about the marriage of Delilah and Orange. I do not know for sure but I believe it must have been a happy home.

At this point I am leaving genealogy and writing about what I learned from my father or got from my own imagination.

I know that Delilah was probably what one would call a "midwife" and was always caring for people who were ill or pregnant. She wasn't home very much. Her husband, Orange, was also away for long periods of time. My father said that Orange would take provisions in a knapsack and sleep on the ground near his campfire while he walked back to Canada to stay for two weeks visiting and helping elderly relatives. He would cross over to Canada on a small ferry at Detroit. This journey meant that his own family was left alone and unprotected for four months from Indian attacks and other perils of the time. The family consisted of six children, three girls and three boys. In order by their ages, Estella, Ernest (my father), Belle, John, Worth, and Edith.

The only thing I can remember daddy telling about their life was that his mother, Delilah, had to leave one afternoon and that she had cautioned her children not to go near the stove while she was gone. Evidently my father was outside and Estella was supposed to be in charge. She and Belle were not too careful. Maybe they were interested in boyfriends or doing their hair but their attentions were elsewhere when John started to chase Worth around the stove. Worth fell on the stove and was badly burned. Fortunately, Edith was a baby and too small to take part.

When mother came home she scolded Estella for not watching them carefully and she punished John severely. Worth had had a fever when he was very small and now this injury added to his poor health. He was never very well and his mind wasn't right at times. He loved his folks and played the violin for hours and in spite of his poor health he grew up, remained single, managed to earn a living for himself as a shoe cobbler and was loved and respected in his community.

Estella was a beautiful woman with dark brown hair and eyes. Worth shared these traits with her. The rest of the family had blue eyes and black hair like their father, Orange. Estella or "Stell" as my father called her was the "belle" of the family and could do no wrong. She married very young and at least four times. There wasn't much love lost between she and my father.

Much to the disgust of the family, Belle married a man in Indiana by the name of Patton. She was practically ostracized. Why, I do not know. Early in her marriage the couple left Indiana by ox team and finally settled in Arkansas. The family heard from her once or twice in later life. The couple had three or four children but outside of that my father did not know and seem to care less. He mentioned her name once or twice and when we were living in Missouri he received a letter that said she had died. He didn't even answer it or show any concern so I do not know her children's names or anything about their lives even though they were my first cousins.

When my father, Ernest, was about nineteen years old, his father, Orange, became ill with the ague, our word for malaria. Indiana around Angola and Pleasant Lake was very swampy and had several lakes especially in Steuben County of which Pleasant Lake was the largest. Mosquitoes thrived. The village where they lived was also called Pleasant Lake. The lakes there now are almost all dried up and gone. Some of the people began to migrate west to escape the dreaded disease and because they heard stories of new rich land. Many families from Steuben County "got the fever" to go west.

Maybe Orange was a second son and could not compete successfully with his older brother A.D. My father always praised and was proud of the successes of A.D.'s children. He often talked of how they grew up to be great violinists, doctors, and ministers. Maybe he told me this to impress me.

Anyway, my grandfather, Orange, decided to take his family and "go west to grow up with the country" and because my father was the oldest son, barely nineteen, he had the responsibility of their wagon and lives on the journey. How many wagons were in the train, I have no idea. Estella and her husband, whose last name was Burnham, and their two year old son, Bob, were a part of the caravan. There was also a family by the name of Carter whose son Otis married my Aunt Edith, the youngest of the Crain children, in later years.

My father kept a diary of the trip in 1878 which he kept in his trunk at home in Missouri. The diary is over a hundred years old and in places is impossible to read clearly. Because it was written in pencil, sometimes the writing is too dim to make out. Parts of it seem slow and uninteresting but others are full of drama, a good picture of the hardships of those times. When he died in 1949 I had to recopy it because of deterioration and the rapidly fading writing.

The following chapter is a copy of the Diary of Ernest Bion Crain from the time the Crain family, (Orange, Delilah, Estella, Ernest, John, Worth, and Edith) left Angola, Indiana to the time they arrived west of Fort Scott, Kansas. The diary does not cover the time of arrival in Wellington, Kansas, because the author ran out of paper a few days before the end of the long journey.

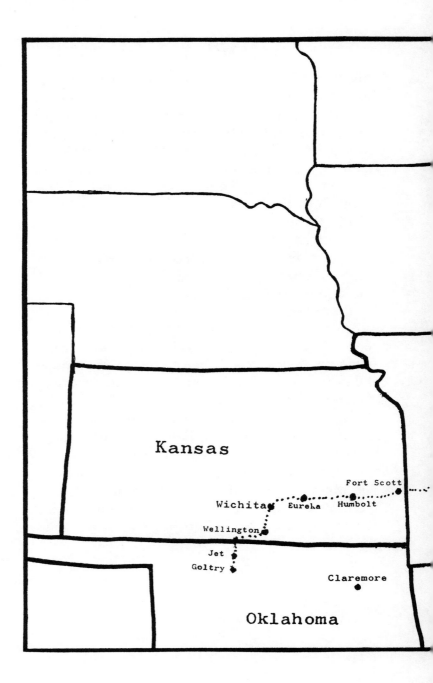

M. Klein 1994

9

THE DIARY OF ERNEST B. CRAIN

September 12 through October 31, 1878

Angola, Indiana
Sept 12, 1878

> We started on September 11, 1878 for a trip to the west with Orange Crain (my father). Traveling all of the 11th, we reached Michigan and Arnold's Corners where we had trouble with the wagon. We completed the repairs by dark and then made it to the Andrews' home to visit P.W. and his wife. We had visiting and business to conduct.

Michigan
Sept 13, 1878

> We left Arnold's Corners at 9:00 a.m. and had a pleasant drive, camping 8 miles from Burr Oak to have our dinner. At half past one o'clock we started on west and reached Burr Oak at 5:00, then continued on to within 3.5 miles of Sturgis to camp for the night. We got supper and made preparations for the night. The weather is pleasant but cool and windy as we passed through nice country today. We are all in good cheer and ready for rations.

Sept 14, 1878

Our camp is here near Sturgis, the weather this morning is very cold, and the surrounding country is very rough, with many oak openings. We left on our journey westward at 7:00 o'clock, and passed through Sturgis at 10:00 o'clock. We stayed one hour and then continued for three miles before pausing for dinner. The surrounding country has little rolling land, with sandy as well as dark soil. At 1:30 o'clock, we left for White Pigeon and crossed the Fawn River, a beautiful stream of water. We stopped in White Pigeon (1100 inhabitants) long enough to shave. Three miles from town we passed through Notaway, a very nice town. We saw beautiful long hedge fences as we passed through Branch County and into St. Joseph.

Sept 15, 1878

We left last night's camp at 7:00 o'clock in the morning and headed for Mottville, one and one half miles from our camp. Leaving Mottville, we crossed the St. Joe River and traveled westward to Union Town for five miles through broken, rough country. It is very much like Steuben County, Indiana here. We came to Cass County, passed through town and took dinner, did a little hunting and shot 2 squirrels and a hawk, and then went on to Adamsville, a distance of 7.5 miles. We crossed Christian Creek, and went on westward for Edwardsburg, four miles from Adamsville, crossing the Chicago and Lake Huron Railroad on the way to Edwardsburg. This is a very pleasant town. We have passed through nice prairie area for about 5 miles with black and sandy soil. We stopped at 5:00 o'clock for the night, got supper and prepared ourselves for the night. The distance traveled today is 26 miles.

Sept 16, 1878

After leaving camp this morning we headed toward Niles, Michigan, 5 miles ahead, a town of 5,000 inhabitants. Continuing northwest we traveled through rough and sandy country. We left the wagon and hunted, going through woods to Berrien Springs, crossing St. Joe River at the same crossing yesterday, traversed the town all over, stayed until sundown, and then went on south 2 miles to camp for the night at Berry Hummerson's.

Sept 17, 1878

Today we are staying in the same place as yesterday. We spent the day in Berrien Springs, staying until 9:00

o'clock and returning to Berry Hummerson's to our camp.

Sept 18, 1878

We left Hummerson's at 9:00 o'clock and arrived at St. Joseph at noon. We put out the team (unhitched them) and walked to the lake shore (Lake Michigan) to go out on the pier for a closer look at the lighthouse. We saw a ship named *Alice Richard* from Manitowoc loaded with iron ore from Michigan mines. We were allowed on board to look around, then left to have dinner. Then we returned to the wharf to see the tug *Daisy Lee*, a pleasure boat from Benton Harbor. Two more steamers appeared from Chicago, one called the *Messinger* and the other the *Carrona*. I wrote and mailed a letter to Indiana and then returned to camp for the night.

Sept 19, 1878

Early in the morning we headed on towards South Bend, Indiana (population 13,000) to pick up friends at the depot there, but could not find them. So we put the team in the barn and went to dinner. Then we returned to the barn to feed them and went to visit the woolen factory. We also went up in a Stand Pipe Tower over 200 feet high, and we saw a splendid sight in every direction. At 4 o'clock I got shaved at the barber shop and 50 minutes later left town headed for the depot and found the friends we couldn't find this morning. We readied the team and started back to camp at nearly sundown. Reached Niles at 8:00 and then Berrien at half-past eleven to retire for the night.

Sept 20, 1878

This morning we got ready to head out but it commenced to rain, so we remained here in the same camp. Three of us went hunting and stayed out until nearly dark.

Sept 21, 1878

This morning we left Mr. Hammerson's place for the west again, and traveled through Buchanan at noon. We stopped long enough to buy crackers, tins of food and cups and traveled for two miles before stopping for dinner. Going on for a few more miles, we stopped and camped at a very pleasant place. We hunted briefly, got a squirrel, and then turned in for the night.

Sept 22, 1878
Indiana

We started on our way at 9:00 o'clock this morning, traveling through Teracopia Prairie, Hamilton, Rolling Prairie, past Carlisle on the left side and Prairie Station on the right, then through Byron. Two miles west of

Byron we camped for supper and camped for the night on the Little Kankakee River.

Sept 23, 1878

We left camp at 7:30 o'clock this morning and traveled west toward LaPorte. We reached there at 8:30 and stayed about a half hour to supply ourselves with provisions. I sent two postals (postcards) back home to friends, then we continued on our way. We passed by Door and Oxbow, and went on toward Westville, a little railroad town 12 miles from LaPorte. We camped for the night 4 miles from Valparaiso, had supper and went to bed.

Sept 24, 1878

Left camp this morning and went through Valparaiso at 9:00 o'clock going west. We passed through Deep River, Crown Point (1800 in habitants) and on for one mile south to camp for the night in the rain. It lasted all night.

Sept 25, 1878

We left at 8:00 in the morning and went on south for 13 miles until noon. I came near having the Ague (a fever with chills). We paused for dinner and went on for about three miles before hauling up (stopping) for a very hard rain shower. Then we continued on through Lowell to State

Road where we camped in a schoolhouse to stay the night. Now I really
have the Ague.

Sept 26, 1878
Illinois

We left the schoolhouse at 8:00 and
stopped at Sherburnville to write two
postals, then continued on to Mo-
mence on the Kankakee River. We
stopped to buy bread (for $.50) and
went on out of town a half mile to
have our dinner. Orange (father), I,
and John went down the Kankakee
for 3 miles and the team continued on
to Kankakee city. We got to the camp
at 7:30 and went to bed.

Sept 27, 1878

We left camp about 7:00 o'clock and
went into Kankakee but I am sick
with the Ague this morning and
stayed in Cap's wagon while the others looked around. I rode all day but
was able to get up and out when we
stopped. We crossed the Kankakee
bridge but did not get as far as
Dwight, 16 miles ahead. We stopped
and camped instead for the night. It
was nice here.

Sept 28, 1878

Started from camp at 9:00 this morning, passed over Grand Prairie to
reach Dwight by 5:00 o'clock. Then
we continued on west for 3 miles and
camped for the night in a barn be-

cause it threatened to rain. Dwight has 1600 people in its town.

Sept 29, 1878

This is Sunday. We left camp about 7:30 as usual and traveled west, soon coming to the town of Odel on our direct route. I was sick with the Ague all forenoon. We stopped near the station of Cayuga for dinner and then continued on to reach Pontiac, the county seat of Livingston County, at 3:00 o'clock. There is a very fine courthouse here in the town square. Leaving Pontiac, we crossed the Vermillian River and drove 5 miles southwest to camp for the night. The weather has been pleasant but the night is very windy.

Sept 30, 1878

It is still windy as we leave camp this morning. We came through the village of Sherborn but did not stop but continued on till noon and stopped for dinner along the roadside. We got off on the wrong road for a short time after dinner, but back-tracked and found the right route. This delayed us just a short while. Lexington lay ahead and we passed through it at 3:00, then on until 5:00 o'clock. We could not find water for the teams, or water for cooking either, but we decided to make do and stop anyway. Fortunately no one was sick today.

Oct 1, 1878

We started on at 5:00 this morning because of a lack of water, but found it about 1 mile down the road. We watered the teams and cooked breakfast, and then headed on towards Bloomington. On the route was the town of Normal and we stopped for a short time to buy a lantern. Out of town about a mile we stopped for dinner. It looked rainy, but we went on for about 2 miles before encountering a terrible storm. We all were soaked through, and as a result spent a cold wet night. There was no dry wood nor good water, so we had a cold lunch and went to bed. One of the towns we passed through was the railroad town of Towanda.

Oct 2, 1878

Nothing unusual occurred today so for once all went well. We found water and cooked breakfast before leaving camp. The day was pleasant and the country in this area was very nice as we passed in sight of two towns. Then on, we went through McLean and into Caswell county.

Oct 3, 1878

We passed a very pleasant night and were up at 3:30 o'clock and ready to start at 7:00. It is a very warm day as we moved on toward the Illinois River. When we were within 10 miles we stopped and had to set up camp because Mr. Crain has been very sick. We found and set up a fine camp site. Today we passed through the town of Delavan.

Oct 4, 1878

Mr. Crain is feeling better this morning so we proceeded on at 7:00 o'clock. The day was so pleasant we hurried on fast and reached the long looked-for Illinois River by 2:30. The cost to cross the bridge was 35 cents for all of us. We crossed quickly, and drove into a grove down river on the left bank to do the washing. By then we were well past the town of Havana in Mason County. The night became rainy and very unpleasant.

Oct 5, 1878

At daybreak all were up and ready to do the work needed, but I was taken with the Ague again. Mr. Crain was sick also. However, the day was pleasant and it cleared up brightly, so we went across the river to get medicine for Ague for those who are sick. It cost 10 cents to cross the bridge. At 5:00 o'clock I rowed over the river in a boat and came back feeling quite well.

Oct 6, 1878

It is Sunday! We prepared to travel on and got started at 9:30. We are all feeling better this morning and went on 5 miles before stopping to dry our clothes and eat dinner. At 1:30 we continued on over very rough country and bad roads. We passed through Summum, a town like Flint, and had to drive up a hill of sandstone stacked ledge upon ledge. Mr. Crain was not feeling well again but we traveled on 3 miles along the Spoon River that flows into the Illinois. The water was very muddy in both rivers. We stopped at 6:00 for the night.

Oct 7, 1878

We started from Camp at 7:00 this morning and traveled towards Astoria, reaching the town about 10:00. Mr. Crain is feeling worse and so am I, so we lay in the wagon all day as we passed through very rough country between Astoria and Rushville. These towns are in Schuyler County. In Rushville we bought Ague medicine from a Dr. Clark, and camped for the night between Astoria and Rushville. The weather was pleasant and Mr. Crain and I felt better after taking the medicine.

Oct 8, 1878

This morning we are up and ready for breakfast but it looks rainy so we are hurrying to get on the road. The rain commenced and the road got so slippery we could not travel, so we pulled into a grove (of trees) and stayed until the storm was over. The Ague is still with me and also with Mr. Crain. He is poorly this morning. We ate our dinner and started off again. We encountered rough roads with steep hills to climb. The weather finally cleared for a time and it was pleasant. At 3:30 o'clock we decided to camp in a grove for the night, and had a thunderstorm before morning.

Oct 9, 1878

This morning we are all feeling better so are able to leave camp at 7:30 o'clock. The rough country continues and the road is very bumpy

Oct 10, 1878

We left this campsite at 7:30 o'clock. All feeling better except Mr. Crain who is feeling worse than yesterday. He is not well at all, very poorly. We reached Camp Point at noon and bought bread and oil. We continued on through the town of Columbus and 3 miles further camped for the night near a schoolhouse. Here we found a man of very poor principle so we could not buy hay enough for the horses, or water enough to use for supper. Then it rained before bedtime so we all slept in the wagons and had a serious night of it because it was very unpleasant and rainy.

Oct 11, 1878
Missouri

This morning it was quite pleasant and made us all feel better. We started out early and drove over rough country of limestone rocks all along the way. We were within three miles of Quincy at 11:00 so we stopped to feed the horses and eat dinner and then continued on to the city. Reached Quincy at 2:00, continued on to reach the great Mississippi River. Drove our teams on board the ferry *Rosa Fayken* to the other side, traveled on five miles and came along the shore of the Meredith River. This is where we lost the basket containing $1.25 in money, revolver, two razors and some other valuable articles. Here we had to pay toll for the team. We ended up camping in a very low place. The water is poor and we all slept in the wagons. We are in Marion County.

Oct 12, 1878

We left camp early to go into the woods to pick up very large hickory nuts. We returned to camp for breakfast and got ready to head towards Palmyra at 8:00 o'clock. The country is rough and river beds are limestone rocks and ledges. We came to a railroad running through a limestone quarry, and then reached the town of

Palmyra, a very nice town with many negroes, at 1:00 o'clock. We stopped for an hour and then went on 1 mile to camp for dinner. It was 3:00 p.m. when we came to within 1 mile of West Ely and camped for the night. It was quite pleasant and all of us felt better after a good supper. It rained before morning.

Oct 13, 1878

This is Sunday! We all felt quite well but it is very unpleasant because of the rain, so we stayed in our wagon until it was over. We were all ready to start out at 7:30 and drove 11 miles before camping for dinner. Mr. Crain is feeling worse and it made it rather unpleasant. We drove west through West Ely, and then on to Monroe City where we bought bread. Water is scarce so we could hardly get enough to cook with. We watered the team in mud holes beside the road. I shot two quail nearby on the prairie. We met 4 teams going east and 4 others going west, so we all camped for the night within sight of each other. Had a very pleasant night of it here in Rockswell County.

Oct 14, 1878

All arose early and felt better than usual, had breakfast and started out at 6:30, traveling toward Paris, a distance of 17 miles. We passed over very rough country, the river bottoms are paved with stone and the water is riley and muddy. We crossed the Salt River and camped within one and a half miles from town. Had our dinner and went into town to buy bread and potatoes, had a shave, and wrote two postals then continued on. We could not find water for the team nor water for cooking. We traveled on and could not find feed for the team until dark. We camped in the Salt River bottom in the woods, and joined company here with 8 more teams going west and 4 teams going east. Paris is in Monroe County, the County Seat. The night was very pleasant.

Oct 15, 1878

It is very pleasant so all rose early to start on the road by 6:30. We traveled toward Middle Grove, a distance of 8 miles, and reached there at 10:00 a.m. The country is rough and stony and water is muddy. We stopped at 12:00 for dinner and then continued on to Renick, a railroad town of not much importance. This country is worse than Indiana. All the water we could get is cistern water. We went 4 miles beyond Rensick and camped for the night. It was very windy, rather disagreeable, and looked like rain, so we slept in our wagons. We are in Howard County.

Oct 16, 1878

All felt well and arose early. We prepared breakfast and got ready to travel. We left camp at 7:00 and headed to Bunker Hill. Arrived there at 10:00. This is not much of a town so we did not stop but continued on. We had a light rain shower and camped on a river bottom for dinner. This is very rough country and the crops are light here in Howard county. We headed on toward Fayette, which is the county seat, and continued on 4 miles more, and camped for the night. I shot 3 quail and then went to bed. In the evening one horse was sick, but he seemed all right in the morning.

Oct 17, 1878

Left camp at daybreak and headed toward Boonville. We came through a town called Franklin and then to Boonville, where we came in sight of the Missouri River, a very muddy stream. We crossed on the ferry *Birdie Brent*, and docked on the other side at a very nice town. There we saw the steamer *Fannie Lewis* docked also. We looked over the area and found it very rough. Further on, Cooper County was a little better with more wheat grown than usual. The country is more level as we drove on west about 8 miles and camped in

a wooded area with 15 other wagons.
There is plenty of water here.

Oct 18, 1878

The night being pleasant all felt well
but Mr. Crain sick again. Left camp
at sunrise for Sedalia, drove through
a small town called Pilot, Grove
County. Nice for a ways, rest very
rough and hilly, almost solid rock and
water scarce, camped at noon, ate
dinner and drove through awful
rough country, stony, crops light,
everything very dear & scarce,
reached Pettit County. Within 8
miles of the town bought some hay
and made preparations for camping
for the night. It was cool but pleasant.

Oct 19, 1878

All arose early for breakfast and prepared to travel towards Sedalia. It
took 1.50 hours to reach town where
we bought provisions, then on to Cal-
houn and five miles out camped for
dinner. The country is nice here and
the town is the county seat of Pettis
County. Going on, we had good roads
from here on towards Clinton, and 27
miles short of town we camped on the
banks of a very muddy river. Good
water is scarce here. The night was
warm, we washed some clothes, and
we camped with 12 teams, some going our way and others returning to

the east. We heard bad reports of la-
bor in Kansas.

Oct 20, 1878

We left camp early. This is Sunday
and we are all feeling better. We
drove towards the town of Windsor in
Henry County. Water is very scarce
yet but crops here look a little better
than usual. We reached Windsor at
10:00 and stopped a little time before
going on to pause for dinner. We were
within sight of a coal bed and the
ruins of a slave plantation.

Oct 21, 1878

We were all up early to go on our way
and passed through the town of Clinton to the town of Lewis where we
stopped to buy corn. Then we continued on and passed a very nice sight, a
coal pit. Here it started to rain and
got very unpleasant. At a town of
3,000 inhabitants (un-named) we met
Eugene Halsted bound for Wichita,
Sedgewick County, Kansas. We made
up our minds to go there also, so we
camped for the night 3 miles out of
town. The next morning we traveled
on with three more teams bound for
the west. We were disappointed
about a school (maybe ahead in
Wichita) so were discouraged about
going on. Very cold and frosty here as
we camped, and wood is scarce. Cap
(Eugene Halsted) went on and left us

to travel on toward Ford Scott, Kansas.

Oct 22, 1878

We did not leave camp as early as we calculated on account of Eugene going back into town. We did finally leave at 7:00 a.m. and passed over some very nice country. We passed a coal mine before the wagon broke down. We managed to tie up the break and continued on into town to a blacksmith shop where the wagon break was repaired. We camped the night on a river bottom where there was wood and good water. The evening was pleasant.

Oct 23, 1878

All up at daybreak to prepare to travel on. It is 6:15. We had very good roads for traveling although some were stony, and by 9:30 there were some rough hills. Coming down a small hill, the clip of the whipple-tree came off and the wagon tongue dropped and broke the wheel. Went to find a wagon shop but could not find one so went on to Johnstown where we camped out for the night. We found a shop but could not get work done until morning. We slept on the ground in a woods and had a very pleasant time.

Oct 24, 1878

Did not get the wagon part repaired until noon, then returned to camp and arrived at 4:00 p.m. We ended up staying in this place for 1 1/2 days before staring on again. We had a splendid time, the night very pleasant.

Oct 25, 1878

We all arose early and as we were all as well as usual, we made preparations for going on towards Papinsville. We were there by noon. Mr. Merill lost his dog so we found him another in Papinsville, a very nice hound. Passed through very nice area, some roads are solid stone, not many hills all prairie. There are not many woods to be seen. We came to the Meridegine River only to find the bridge condemned. We had to drive down the bank, a very bad hill to descend. All had to get out of the wagons, we chained the wheels down and it was difficult getting up the hill on the other side. Then we continued on toward Ball Town and passed over some very nice country, going on until dark before finding wood and water. The dog got run over and it hurt him very badly. The night was very cool and dark. We camped in a woods near a creek called Little Osage. Its water is the best we found in the state of Missouri.

Oct 26, 1878

Kansas

Left camp early in the morning and it is damp and rainy. We prepared for the day's travel and wended our way toward Ball Town. Then on toward Fort Scott. We camped on the Marlin River and the water was so low we could see the bottom, paved with stone nicer than the hands of nature could produce. Here we passed over the finest prairie we went through in our travels. We are now in Kansas. We went six miles and at 3:00 camped on the banks of a splendid river whose water is clearer than in Missouri. Had plenty of wood and a splendid camping ground. We had to go into Ft. Scott for bread. The night was very cold and dark, and we were told that in Kansas City they had 8 inches of snow. We had a little flurry here.

Oct 27, 1878

We did not hurry this morning. Did not start out until 10:00 because it is Sunday. We had to pass through the river because there is no bridge. The river banks on both sides are very steep. We drove on into Fort Scott and spent half an hour to get provisions. This town is in Bourbon

County with a population of 16,875, very flourishing. Leaving town, we took a west course for Wichita until almost dark. We found a spring and wood, so camped there for the night on the prairie near a gully. We see immigrants going west more than ever.

Oct 28, 1878

At 2:00 a.m. this morning all were up early on account of horse thieves. The horses were tied to the wagon and we were sleeping quietly when the silence was disturbed by the barking of the dogs, and some whispering between the parties. They got one horse 15 yards from the wagon and the second horse untied and ready to leave, but were discovered. We chased and shot at but did not catch them. But we remained up the rest of the night and made preparations for starting early. As we went on we traveled over some nice prairie land, high mounds, and soil as black as your hat. We could see houses 20 miles off, and the country through Bourbon was nice and rolling. We passed through Union Town, very small, and stopped to get warm. This is very cold country but we had a very pleasant time here. Had to buy wood to burn at night. We also had a breakdown, the Healstean wagon, so had to put up in camp to repair. The night was pleasant and there was no disturbance with the horse thieves, but we watched all night for them to be sure.

Oct 29, 1878

All rose early and feeling quite well, we got ready to move on. Mr. Crain talked of getting a house and not going on further west, but finally concluded to move on with the rest. We were all feeling out of humor and so did not get ready to leave camp until noon. We moved on toward Humbolt in Allen County, a very rough land on and along the Walnut River. We camped and went hunting for a short time but did not shoot anything. After dinner we started for Humbolt and went through very fine prairie country. We drove within 2 miles of town and camped beside a stream where we got water, but very little wood. We suffered some from the cold and had to eat a cold supper.

Oct 30, 1878

We watched all night for horse thieves so were out early and ready to start for Humbolt after we ate breakfast. Arriving in town, we bought provisions and remained until about 10:00 o'clock. We headed on and crossed the Neosho River. Near here we almost came near taking (buying) a farm, but did not. The area is growing better all the time. The day was very windy and tore the cover from the wagon box. We crossed Owl Creek and camped for dinner in Woodson County. As we continued on it was very cold and we suffered very much. We crossed a nice prairie, hills and hollows stony and rough, water nice and clear. I went on ahead 3 miles and built a fire and got a supply of wood ready. The teams came into camp, all very cold. Worthy (brother) is very sick, but other than his being ill, we had a nice time.

Oct 31, 1878

This night was the coldest one we have had on our journey and we've had a rough time keeping warm. We watched all night for horse thieves but were not molested. We tried to prepare breakfast but it was so cold we could not eat, so we started early towards Toronto. The country here is nice. We forded the Verdigro River and passed along through land all rolling. We passed two coal beds and hear coal was worth $1.50 a ton. There is no wood but on the river bottoms. We camped along the Walnut River in Greenwood County Kansas for dinner. Then continued on to arrive at Eureka at dark. There we could not get much wood. It is windy and cold and we are suffering from the cold. We watched the horses but no distrubance from the horse thieves this cold night.

The diary notes end here.

Note: Edited for easier reading.

Paid out on material for Western Trip

Canvas and cover 1.35
1 lb. Nails...04
5 1/2 doz. Screws 20
1 shave and cards...........................23
3 lbs crackers 7 loaves of bread.....50
Beer and peanuts 35
Cakes and grubbs? 10
Postage stamps & ? 25
Hay for horses 20
? and others articles.......................25
? corn...20
Total (I counted)..........................2.67
       Diary looks like $4.27

In account
?butter 2 lbs....................................30
1/4 lb. Powder 30
2 valferaiso bread...........................25
Seven postales back 12
Bread 10 loaves 50
Sent 4 postales 04
Onions & ? 15
Medicine for ague..........................75
Grapes...20

Paid towards a lantern 1.00
& in Delhoom ? Paid 40
& Havana Paid...............................60
Medicine for the ague 85
Medicine for Ruchville
of Dr. Clark.................................2.00
Total...7.46

Butter in Crownpoint.....................35
Bread & crackers............................30
Fresh pork 15
Ammunition 30
1 lb. of coffee 30
1 box of matches............................05
Wrote 3 postales............................03
1/2 gal molasses.............................20
Bread 25
1 stove..10
Pen and pencil...............................10
Postales...10
Molasses 25
Bread and candy 45
Candy...05

16.85	14.04	3.70
18.36	4.27	2.93
35.21	18.36	7.46

Eggs per dozen 10
Corn 25
Biscuits and candy........................55
Pork 12 lbs, at 5 cts.......................60
Bo't some pecans 10
Total...1.60

J. W. Herdon

Near park city 7 miles north & miles west of Wichita. Met & camped with him on the bank of the Little Osage and he also said that arrangements we could make with you would be satisfactory with him.

Ginger cake and other articles of provisions to amt.	....	30
Pork	....	60
Bread	....	50
Other Articles	....	20
Ammunition	....	40
Gun Screw	....	10
Apples	....	10
Razor and strap and brush	....	1.85
Total	....	20.85

Note: J. W. Herdon and Eugene Halstead also made the run into the Indian Territory and settled near the Crains. Eugene later went to Goltry, Oklahoma in the territory. The couple had two children, Altha Halstead Thomas and Elgin Halstead. Eugene died in a nursing home in his home town in western Michigan in the 1940's. J. W. Herdon lived and died near Jet Oklahoma Territory in the nineteen forties.

KANSAS

The family with Eugene Halstead went on beyond Wichita and settled south of there at either Wellington or Caldwell, Kansas.

I am not sure which place but my father told me about working near Wellington and Harper, Kansas. He never mentioned it to me but I have learned from genealogy research that a communal colony or community was established there with many settlers from the east including the states of Indiana, New York, Illinois, and others. They purchased land and built farms and homes.

The journey had begun on September 12, 1878 and the last day as recorded in the diary was Oct. 31, 1878, a period of approximately 48 days or about eight weeks. They eventually settled in Harper County, Kansas. I have no data but I would guess that as my father often talked about life in Harper County.

Harper County is the border County to Oklahoma and approximately thirty to forty miles from Wichita. Most of the company probably settled close together because most of them were together in Oklahoma after the Cherokee Strip opening. They were like a colony in north Kansas and Oklahoma.

They were all farmers and probably tilled farm land near a settlement. My father often talked about Harper County, but I don't recall anything outstanding except that he had found a bachelor farmer near Wellington who hired him for a period of two or three years and that he lived and worked in the man's home. This man must have been a successful settler as daddy was always telling about what an excellent cook he was and how he conducted his farm. Daddy enjoyed living there and working for him.

Daddy's baby sister Edith told me in later years that she remembered playing in a buffalo wallow as a child. Life was hard for youngsters. They had no playthings like dolls and toys and the only fun they could find was wading barefoot in the buffalo wallows after a spring freshet or digging in the hot dust in the summer. She probably spent much of her time later working in the home or fields with her father and brothers. The oldest child, Estella (Stell) was married and may have lived with her husband and son, Bob, on an adjoining farm or even in the Crain household.

If the reader doesn't know what a buffalo wallow is, it is easy to explain. There were large herds of buffalo on the prairies and in the spring the buffalo wallow may have been a dusting place and later if the hole began to dry up the buffalo would wallow to keep cool and wet their coats. The oil and fuzz from their hides would get into the mud and when the wallow finally dried up in the hot summer sun it became a dust wallow until the next season.

When the family had lived in the Kansas settlement about nineteen years, word came out of Washington that the government was going to open the Cherokee lands in Oklahoma for settlement to the white people. Orange became restless and wanted to move on. About three months before the actual date for the opening, members of the settlement decided to go into the territory to pick out a suitable place for a homestead. Orange, along with his three sons, Ernest (my father), John and Worth, traveled around in an old farm wagon through the Indian country and decided where they would like to settle. Other families did the same. It was easy since the Indian Territory was just across the state line from Harper County.

The Crains had several adventures on their last trip into the territory. Once they ran out of provisions and one of them got lost from the original campsite. At the campsite they had nothing but dry beans and coffee to eat for three days. Finally, they made their choice of land and returned home safely.

Negotiations with the United States government and the Creek and Seminole tribes were successfully concluded in 1889, and at noon on April 22 the land was opened up to the public. A race for the best lands and town sites ensued, as nearly 50,000 persons flooded the Territory the first day.

On March 2, 1890, the Federal Government established the Territory of Oklahoma, which consisted of lands in the southern part of the region, and the western portion of the Indian Territory, in addition to the panhandle strip north of Texas.

In 1892 the Cherokees sold to the United States government their western territorial extension, known as the "Cherokee Outlet", and in 1906 they disbanded their nation and became citizens of the United States.

Word went out that all families desiring to make the run were to dispose of all their lands and belongings except what they would need in their new home. They were to pack their food, clothing, farm tools, and furniture such as chests and beds in a Conestoga wagon. This necessitated tethering horses and cows to the wagons as well as hanging wash tubs and chicken crates, etc. on the outside. (Conestoga wagons are not very big.) The Crain family already had some experience with these wagons.

In order to obtain material for a description of "the Run into the Territory" my father suggested Uncle Otis Carter, who had married his youngest sister Edith and lived in Perryton, Texas, could help me. Uncle Otis' family had been in the original trip from Indiana.

When I came home from Michigan, mother and I went to Perryton to see Uncle Otis and Aunt Edith Carter. Uncle Otis was elderly at that time and forgetful, but I spent some time with him and he told me the following things:

Participating families had to have all their possessions in a wagon, their stock tied to the wagon and be on the starting line ready to go at the signal of the gun shot. Harper and Summer County, Kansas were the scenes of the run. The wagons were to line up on the starting line on the border between Oklahoma and Kansas.

All was excitement and expectation. Perhaps some feared that they might not make the run safely. Some wagons overturned, wrenched and their occupants killed near the starting line. The noise and confusion was breathtaking.

I don't know how many wagons the Crain and Carter families had but they took a straight dash ahead and then veered to the southwest. All were looking for a new life and praying for safety and God's blessing.

The incentive for "making the run" was to obtain a virgin, fertile tract of land at the unbelievable sum of five dollars an acre in cash with the option to purchase 120 acres and vow to live upon that land and improve it for the next ten years as they saw fit. Perhaps the adventure was what appealed to some but to have the opportunity to obtain fresh virgin soil at such an attractive price was a gift from God.

OKLAHOMA TERRITORY

Our group was very happy and satisfied to find land within a few miles of each other with no mishap and near the places they had chosen after their trip into the territory the summer before. The county in which they obtained land was called Alfalfa County reestablished from old Woods County.

My father's land was located half way between what later was to become two towns, Goltry and Jet, Oklahoma. To the east of my father's choice of land about five miles was the land chosen by his younger brother, John. Uncle John's choice was a little lower and there was a wet weather stream flowing near it. My grandfather bought a farm about one half mile to the northwest of my father's place which was called the school quarter. School quarter land was a portion of land that the money from its sale was to go to the county for providing a free school for the children. My grandfather purchased the land for his youngest son, Worth, who was not old enough to buy land. Later Worth inherited it and all of the family except daddy and Uncle John lived on the school quarter. Uncle Otis and Aunt Edith obtained a homestead about five miles south of my father's place and improved it.

The first thing my father had to consider and do after making his choice was to find the corner stones on the land. Since that part of the

Cherokee Strip had only red and brown soil and no rocks, that seemed simple. When the land was surveyed, the corner stones were large imported rocks brought in and buried to mark the land.

In order to lay claim, it was necessary to mark the spot and report the land claim to the authorities at Guthrie, which was a small frontier town many miles from where father's place was located. After reporting and proving his spot he then had to start building fences to enclose it. Most of his family and friends accomplished that, but he hunted for days for the northwest corner and could not find it. He was so discouraged he almost gave up but that was the land he liked and wanted most.

His father and brother, John, had tried to help but to no avail. Most of the land around him had been taken up, so one night he went back to his campsite with feelings of frustration and a desire to give it all up. After a late meal (such as it was) he laid down on his pallet and prayed for help and guidance.

Along in the night he had a peculiar dream that if he would go to a single live cottonwood tree growing along the west side of a spring branch (wet and running with a small creek in the spring and dried up and sere in the summer) and pace off fifty feet straight north (by compass) and begin to dig he would find the marker.

When he woke up the sun was shining so he did his chores – caring for his team and having breakfast but he couldn't believe what he had dreamed. Nevertheless he had tried everything else and it hadn't worked, so he went over to the cottonwood tree, a forlorn tree that was having a hard time staying alive, and paced off the distance. Then he began to dig.

While he was digging his brothers, John and Worth, and his father, Orange, came to see if he was alright. He told them of his dream and soon with their help he dug a little deeper and found the cornerstone rock. They thanked God for guiding them to the spot.

The next day they made plans to go to Guthrie to file his claim, with one of the family staying on the property until he could return, and begin operations. It took several days to make the trip and return with a wagon, team and supplies. He had to buy fencing supplies and provisions for living as much as he could carry on a wagon. Later the family learned to go to another little town in the opposite direction called Pondcreek. Both towns became famous later as pioneer towns in the Cherokee Strip. Pondcreek never grew but still remains a wide place in the road. Guthrie became the historical site of the Cherokee Strip.

As soon as his claim was established and paid for, he returned safely and began to fence in the hundred and twenty acres. He also made plans for a "soddie" roof over his head.

There was a dry arroyo on the east side of his claim with a low place where giant willow trees were growing. On the steep side of this arroyo he dug out a space in the bank for a small room about 15 x 10 feet in size. He reinforced this hole with wooden 2 x 4's and put in a front door and wonder of wonders, a glass window and screen which he had bought in Guthrie. Then on the top he constructed a chimney, possibly a pipe of some kind, and covered the wooden roof with sod.

When I was a child about 6 years old, I was allowed to explore for myself, accompanied by my dog Poodle, and I can remember going to this place and seeing that most of the wood had rotted, the window was broken, the wooden beams had rotted and the front had fallen in. I was afraid of rattlesnakes and the unknown so I didn't stay there very long. There is still a vivid picture in my mind of a cave on the side of the deep red soil of the arroyo.

I can remember my mother telling me I was not to go northeast of our door step and when I asked, "Why?" I was told that I might fall in an old well and be drowned or be unable to get out. In later years my mother took me to the place where my father had dug a well and after he no longer had a use for it he had covered it with a wooden top. We found the well all right but we could not go near it because the walls were beginning to fall in and the top was rotting. That part of the farm just above the arroyo was never used and was out of bounds to me.

In later years I dreamed of falling into a well and when I reached the bottom it would be a barn. I wonder about it. It was always a nightmare.

Huge clumps of buffalo grass grew on the prairie and few trees; a small cottonwood in an arroyo could survive the hot, dry summers. In the small stream beds willow trees grew and survived and sometimes one would find a wild plum thicket. Housewives would gather the fruit and make wild plum jelly. The plums were bitter but they did make the best jelly one ever tasted.

Occasionally we would find a tumbleweed patch and a few desert–like wild flowers in the spring but mostly soap weed (Yucca) would grow and bloom in the early summer. On a hot day we would find one or two huge rattlesnakes coiled up under the soap weed to avoid the hot summer sun. The big green stalks of yellow white flowers were beautiful in the pasture but we would always avoid getting too close to the plant for the danger beneath it.

I remember hearing my father say that after working all day in the field he would water and feed his team and then come to his "soddie" built in the arroyo and the first thing he would do was to take the bedding off his built–in cot to see if any rattlesnakes were curled up in it. Sometimes he would find one on the floor under his stove or table. The rattlesnakes would crawl around in the sod on the roof and eventually find a passage down into the cool interior. They were always a threat to the settlers and father always carried a revolver to protect himself.

Oklahoma's best crop in those days was rattlesnakes and prairie dogs. The prairie dog is a small brown creature like a chipmunk without the furry tail. It would burrow into the ground and make many deep, long passage ways under the sod.

Sometimes a prairie dog town would have almost a hundred inhabitants. They lived underground and a lookout would often sit on top of a mound to watch for food and to protect the home. It was a common sight to see one sit on top of the mound and bark at moving objects. If we came near, the prairie dog would watch and then plop down in the hole just when we thought we would be able to catch him. Then he would probably grin at us for our efforts. Once they built a town it was almost impossible to destroy it.

I can remember seeing one large town when I went back to Oklahoma in the 30's. It was one of the few left. There was a small one in the pasture south of our house but my father gradually destroyed it by plowing it up several times and turning his range cattle onto that pasture.

Rattlesnakes and prairie dogs were good friends. The snakes used the town for protection from the elements and they often lived in the deep channels with the prairie dogs. The dogs did not seem to mind that and you would find the two living together and liking each other. Why, I do not know.

The hot dry summers with no food, and farmers destroying the prairie dog towns, took many years.

There were also coyotes, jack rabbits, and wolves. My pet dog Poodle almost killed himself chasing jack rabbits. That was his favorite sport.

After my father built the soddie in the bank of the arroyo, he began to build a fence around the 120 acres and then planned for wheat and corn fields and pasture land, a hog lot, a meadow for hay, a barn, granary, and eventually a house. It took hours of hard work in a hot summer sun, sometimes with little rainfall, and in the winter snow with biting cold northern winds. It was a hard life with few pleasures.

Since we were in what came to be called "Tornado Alley" my family experienced hot winds and often "twisters". I once heard father say he stood in his field and watched a tornado cloud to the south touch down and plow a path a mile wide and five miles long, destroying everything in its path except the land.

When the Crains had been farming their homesteads for about four years, father was called out of bed suddenly by family members and told that his father, Orange, was very ill. He went immediately to the schoolquarter homestead and found his father very ill indeed with a kidney ailment and upset stomach. Orange lived only a half hour after he arrived.

Since there was no expectation of death, the Crain children "chipped in" and bought a family lot in the Timberlake Cemetery near a town named Helena, Oklahoma. My father was the oldest son in the family, so the title to the lot was made out in his name and he paid the taxes on the lot until his death many years later. No one else in the family ever took any responsibility except for wanting to be buried there. After his death I inherited the title and paid the bills until finally I took out perpetual care on the lot. I went back in the forties and found it in excellent condition and one of the most beautiful rural cemeteries I had ever seen.

The reason for the title Timberlake Cemetery is that it was a high mesa on red land near a lake. Maybe you cannot feature a lake in Oklahoma existing but it did.

When the settlers came in it became a sort of summer resort. As the land was settled and plowed for farming there was a change in the seasons through the years and finally a change came about in the earth's interior and the underground streams that fed the lake were cut off. The lake dried up, the trees died, and settlers ceased to come there and enjoy its coolness and comfort. The lake became dry and arid just like that part of Oklahoma.

After my grandfather's sudden death, the family carried on as best they could. Orange Crain had been the monarch of the family and had made all the decisions. It was difficult, but my father became head of the group.

It was about a half mile from grandfather's soddie to daddy's and it must have been a difficult walk for my grandmother but she wanted to do what she could for my father. As I think back she and my father must have been very close and it took this death to bring out the relationship. Occasionally I can remember daddy would mention something about his mother but he seldom spoke of his father except to say that he was very stern and strict and unbending in his decisions. My father didn't know it but he was the "spitting image" of his father, even resembling him in coloring and body makeup.

Working and farming a homestead is a strenuous life and if one does it alone, is a big undertaking with nothing done except what one does oneself. My father often got discouraged and yet that was the only life he knew.

His mother felt sorry for him and wanted to help, so she would bake two or three times a week and carry fresh bread to him, often trying to have a meal ready for him at the noon hour. He had that to look forward to each day but it didn't last very long for about a year after grandfather's death, grandmother took suddenly ill and died in a few hours. Daddy was left an orphan so to speak although he was past forty years old and so he began to think that maybe marriage was the answer.

I have one more rattlesnake story to write before I can go on to the marriage. One season daddy was out plowing the southwestern field for wheat and that morning he had forgotten to take his gun with him. He was plowing in the middle of the field and plowed into the middle of a big rattlesnake den before he realized it. When the horses began to whinny he became aware of rattlesnakes coming toward him and his team from all directions. Horses are deathly afraid of rattlesnakes and he almost froze from fright but he had to do something quickly. Looking around he saw his neighbor Hulsey coming out of his hut on the south adjoining homestead. He started to yell for help. As it happened the neighbor heard him and ran back for his gun. He ran across the plowed field quickly and he got there in time to save dad and his horses from the snakes. Both of them were shook up and vowed they would try to be more cautious. That was the closest call my father ever had and he would be visibly shaken whenever he told the story.

MARRIAGE

Daddy had a friend by the name of Rose, who had come to Oklahoma by way of Republic, Missouri. One day that friend came over to the homestead to visit him and in the course of the visit daddy said, "I am just about to give up. I love this homestead so much but I just don't feel that I can go on day after day with hard work, coming in at night dog tired with no food prepared and sometimes I just go to bed without eating a decent meal. I never did have to cook at home with my big family and I just feel that I can't go on living this way."

Mr. Rose looked at him and said, "I know what you mean. You need a woman to help you. Why don't you marry one of these young girls that come to the Saturday night dances? I think they would jump at the chance to marry an older man with a farm and a future."

Daddy replied, "I have thought about that but I don't want a young dancing partner. I want a woman who knows how to cook and will work beside me indoors and out, one who really knows how to work."

Mr. Rose thought a while and then replied, "I know just the woman for you. She is a widow, comes from a very poor big family that has no money, no real home, a drunken father, and has helped to support that family to keep them from starving. She has no education, no money, no home really. She married a man who was too

old for her with three grown and married children. He finally died about a year ago. Now she
is working in the kitchen of a miner's hotel,
takes her wages (about five dollars a week)
home and her father either demands it or takes
it so she has nothing to live for. She is a good
woman and would be thankful for a home of her
own and a husband to care for. I have known
her for many years and she is a good woman. I
will give you her name and address. She lives
in Missouri close to my old home."

So he gave father the address of Maudie
Owens Kerr living near Marionville, Missouri.

My father accepted the address, wrote to my
mother and although she could hardly write her
name she managed to read his letters and answer them.

In the meantime, my father began to build a
two room house on the bank of the arroyo above
the dug out.

About a year later he wrote to Maudie and
told her he was coming to Missouri to see her.
That was possible because the Frisco Railroad
had just been built going through the little
town of Goltry, Oklahoma, to Enid, to Tulsa,
and then on through Springfield, Missouri.

Maudie did not dare tell her father until the
night before that he was coming but she packed
her trunk and had all her belongings ready.

The next morning my mother, her only
brother, and her youngest sister went in a
spring wagon to meet the train at Marionville.
Her mother could not go and her father was so
angry at her he would not.

Her brother was kind and friendly as always but the youngest sister cried most of the way because she was going to lose her best friend.

In the afternoon the couple took a half mile walk through the woods to the spring branch so that mother could bring back water for the family's daily meals. That was their only source of water.

At the spring my father proposed to her and with trembling heart she agreed to go back to Oklahoma with him.

Daddy asked her father for her hand in marriage as was the custom in those days but her father was most ungracious.

The next morning her only brother took the couple to the railroad station to board the train at Marionville. There were two passenger trains each way every day, one in the morning and one in the evening.

The couple boarded the train at Marionville and got off at the next station west, Carthrage a county seat. Here they went to the courthouse, bought a marriage license and went across the hall to the office of the county judge. He summoned his wife for a witness and they were married. After dinner at the local hotel, they boarded the train for the long journey to Goltry, Oklahoma.

My mother had worked so hard that she was run down. She only weighed about 90 pounds. Because of the hard work and excitement she started to menstruate on the train. She was not dressed for it so she had to ask her new husband to take her suitcase down from the rack so she could get some fresh clothes and then to walk behind her to the ladies room so passengers on the train wouldn't see the spots on her dress. She was also afraid of spotting the chair. Her husband seemed to understand and tried to help her but she never got over that embarrassing experience.

When they arrived in Goltry, father had his team and wagon readied and taken out of the hotel shed and the couple drove five miles to the new two room house on the bleak prairie.

Mother soon set to work to make the new home as comfortable as possible. She had one problem. Father had a big black pet cat who would come to the house occasionally. Daddy called the cat to come and get his food. The cat had never seen a woman before and he took one look at my mother, let out a howl of distress and ran to the buggy shed where father had to take his food. He never came to the house again, but occasionally mother could coax him to eat his food in her presence in the buggy shed. The couple laughed many times over the incident. That old black cat died of a broken heart.

The next day, Uncle John, daddy's brother, was evidently curious and came to see them.

Afterwards he made the remark, "Ern has married a good woman. Look at her hands. She knows how to work."

Daddy's brothers and sisters were never very friendly to mother because they had counted on the fact that daddy would never marry and they would inherit the homestead. Mother always grieved over that fact.

Uncle John was a happy–go–lucky sort of man, never worrying much about the future and treated her best of all her in–laws, and she never forgot that.

The couple went to Goltry for doctor's services, banking needs, food and to attend the Oddfellows and Rebeccas Lodges. Mother entered into the Rebecca activities with misgivings but she soon got over it and enjoyed making friends.

Mother was a good cook and assumed the strenuous duties of a prairie farm. Her family, mother and sisters, were expert gardeners at home in Missouri. They had to be to keep alive and so she felt that she could not live without a garden, even in sun broiled dry Oklahoma. Daddy changed his hog lot to a lower place in the arroyo and dug up the old lot so she could have a garden. She was delighted but soon found that Oklahoma wouldn't produce some of the vegetables she was used to growing. She did have good luck with cucumbers in the rich hog lot soil, and she never forgot to tell about the wonderful cucumbers she raised and pickled for winter use.

There were many things the couple did not agree on and one was onions. Mother loved fried onions. Daddy liked raw onions sliced and covered with vinegar. The odor from fried onions would make Daddy deathly sick so mother would wait until he had to take the wagon for supplies and would be gone for several hours.

Then she would have a great treat of fried onions. She always took care that the odor was
out of the house before he returned. As time
went on he grew used to fried onions and after I
grew up he used to ask Mother to fry them for
him so we had fried onions at least once a week.
Maybe that is why I love fried potatoes and onions.

He also liked beef and since part of his
homestead was a cattle ranch, we never failed
to have beef. He never lost his liking for beef
steak and mother for pork, (she was raised on
it) and sometimes there was a disagreement.
All so–called light bread was homemade.
Mother baked bread one or two times a week
much to daddy's delight. He always said that
mother was a good cook and that is the only
thing I ever remember hearing him brag about.

A DAUGHTER AND A DOG

Of course, a family was the next question. Daddy, like most men, wanted a son to help him on the homestead, so mother agreed to it against her will. She came from a big family which would have starved without her mother. My mother was considered too old and frail in those days (27 years old), to bear a child. My parents were married September 3, 1903, and I appeared on the scene September 18, 1904.

Mother worked hard but she did have some comforts and good food that year. What she liked most was oranges. So, during her pregnancy daddy would often go with his team and wagon into Jet or Goltry for oranges. In those days oranges were almost impossible to get but he did find a few.

Mother was alone and away from her family so the couple made arrangements for her mother to come from Missouri to take care of her. The doctor was Tom Rhodes from Goltry, an old family doctor for many in that part of the territory and one whom daddy had known for a long time. Considering the times, he was one of the best doctors in the country. Mother and the doctor did not know about dieting so I was a ten pounder from a mother who had never weighted over a hundred pounds her whole life. Of course I did not come out head first and I ended up an instrument baby which tore my mother's body (no cesareans in those days).

My mother lived but when I was dressed Dr. Tom told my father that if mother ever had another child she would die. When he heard the circumstances he made a solemn pledge to all that there would never be anymore children. That is the reason I never had any brothers or sisters. I do not know how the couple survived the crisis but they did and were happy and content.

I was named Ada after Dr. Tom's wife and Elizabeth after my father's only aunt. His only aunt was named after queen Elizabeth I of England. So what a character I had to try to live up to!

In the spring after my mother became pregnant she and daddy went over to spend the day with my Uncle John and Aunt Alice. Uncle John had a pet dog who had just given birth to several puppies and Uncle John gave one of the little puppies to mother. She carried the sleeping puppy home on her lap. He was a brown and white mixture, half British Bull and half Shepherd, an awful combination, and he lived up to his breeding. Mother called the dog Whippets or Poodle. Daddy and I called him Poodle. He was a real character. When mother and I were alone Poodle stayed at the house with us for protection from dago peddlers, and he did hate dago peddlers. All mother had to do was call the dog, open the screen door, and the peddler would jump over the big woven wire gate and disappear down the road. Peddlers got to be a nuisance in those days.

In the summer Poodle always slept on the porch steps and at night the coyotes loved to come up and nibble his toes. Then he would chase them through the orchard and come back to sleep on the step. Sometimes the racket would be so loud that daddy would get up, get his gun, and kill or chase the coyotes away.

Mother trained the dog to take care of me when she had to let me outdoors. He was my constant companion. Often when there was the danger of a rattlesnake Poo would push me to the side and fight the rattlesnake. Poo hated rattlesnakes and he must have had a strong instinct for protecting us. I have often thought he could smell a snake several feet away.

Poodle always favored mother and me over daddy. Daddy had a big water tank and windmill about a quarter mile from the house. Afterwards he dug a well and put a windmill close to the doorstep so mother wouldn't have to carry a stick in her hand for protection and a pail of water in the other.

When Poodle had grown older daddy was cleaning out his water tank one day and called him to keep the cattle away from the tank until he had finished. Poodle was a smart dog. He obeyed daddy and kept the cattle back while he completed the job. Daddy was proud of him. The next day, later in the afternoon, daddy heard the cattle bellowing and went to investigate. He found Poodle obeying orders and not letting the cattle come to the tank to drink. Some of the cattle were in pretty bad shape. Evidently Poodle had kept them away for some time. My father didn't often lose his temper. He was usually a very quiet, calm person but this time he got angry. He grabbed a whip and almost killed Poodle. He finally cooled down and put the dog in the buggy shed where he lay bruised and bleeding.

The next morning mother went out to take food to the dog but he was still in bad shape. For 2 or 3 days we thought he would not live. Daddy was sorry for his loss of temper. Mother fed the dog and finally coaxed him to come to the house. He never forgot the whipping. Daddy took him out to the pasture to help him bring the cattle in. From then on Poodle would go with daddy when he was called but never again would he watch or drive the cattle. He would go with daddy and be friends but he always followed behind him. He would obey daddy in other ways but he kept out of the pasture.

Poodle loved to follow the horses and buggy to Jet. He never would ride with us but always preferred to trot behind. Daddy would tell him to guard the buggy and he would lay down under it and no one except our family could go near it or the horses.

When I was about three or four years old, my mother wanted to walk to the mailbox to get the mail. At that time we had begun to receive our mail through a rural route, a new idea in the Cherokee Strip. We thought we were all in "Seventh Heaven" although we had to walk about a half mile to reach the mailbox. Mother always had to do that task if daddy was working the field. That particular July day was a hot one. Mother was tired and she called daddy to stay close and she would leave me at the house because she knew I would get hot and tired and she would have to carry me which was a little too much for her. She carefully explained to me that I could not go because she could not carry me. I refused to go along with her plans and she finally had to spank me. I had a mind of my own so I promptly threw a tantrum. She fussed with my stubbornness until daddy heard the noise and came to the house to see what was going on. I had made up my mind and she could not convince me, so he promptly went out to the buggy shed and brought back his buggy whip. I would not give in so he gave me some cutting licks across my rear until I decided to give up. Mother went on to the mailbox, came back, and cried all night. When she was gone, I was told that when either my father or mother spoke to me I was to mind or else. Daddy knew I took after him and was stubborn. From that time on whenever he told me to do something I did it promptly. I think I was afraid of him so I minded him without any back talk. He knew he had to conquer my spirit and he did. He never spanked me or whipped me but once after that and that was when I was sixteen years old. My mother was very angry and she told him if he ever touched me that way again she would leave him. She did not, and the two never spoke of it again that I know of. However, the incident affected my life.

Soon after that I fell in some tall grass and broke my right arm. We did not know that the arm was broken but I fussed and the next morning my parents took me to Goltry to see Dr. Tom. My arm had been broken the previous afternoon and was not set until almost noon the next day so I had trouble adjusting to it. As a result I could not use my right arm well. My teachers in grade school tried unsuccessfully to get me to write with my right hand and I grew up to be left–handed in all I did. My father said that his father was left–handed and that when he threw a ball it did not look as if he could hit the side of a barn door but he always did. He thought that maybe I took after my grandfather Crain. Maybe I did but I also had some left–handed relatives on my mother's side of the family.

When I was more than six years old, I contracted typhoid fever and was very ill. Dr. Tom Rhodes came out in his buggy many times to see me. He had our drinking water tested and the place inspected. He did all he could considering the medical knowledge of that time but he could not find the answer to his question of where I had picked up the germ and no one else in the area had the disease at the time. I was so ill that I had to learn to walk again and my legs became too large after that. Mother always said that typhoid always settled in one's system some place and that my large legs were the result of it.

I remember one incident while I had the disease. I had begun to recover and move around the house and was not allowed to have anything solid to eat. Mother fed me barley water and other foods that she could liquefy. She and daddy were picking some early ripe peaches from the little orchard he had planted and tended. Mother was canning them for winter use and they were going to pick them before lunch. They told me very carefully what they were going to do and I was not to touch any food until they got back. I was so hungry I could not resist, so I waited until they were in the peach orchard before I went to the stove and took a small boiled potato out of the kettle and ate it. When they came back with the peaches, by instinct Mother knew I had eaten something I should not have so I had to tell her what I had done. The two were so frightened that daddy called the doctor (we had an old–fashioned wall telephone by that time). My parents were both sacred to death, and I was too by that time. The doctor came and stayed for several hours with us but I did not show any signs of illness. He concluded that the boiled potato was soft enough that it had not hurt me. After that I had to go to the peach orchard with them. Daddy didn't say much but that was a fright he never forgot and he insisted that we have a telephone. Telephones were a rarity and a plaything in those days.

LIFE IN THE STRIP

Daddy had four horses, Old Ed, Jane, Pet, and a buckskin pony named Red. Old Ed was the oldest and led the other horses. She loved to take the bit in her mouth and daddy couldn't hold her. She was always tense and looking for something to shy at but she was the best work horse he had. He would hitch her and Jane to the buggy to go to Jet and she would have to be prodded as she was lazy. Any little movement would set her into motion, perhaps a jackrabbit would suddenly pop up or another team would pass the buggy. Then Old Ed would show off. She would suddenly shy to one side, whinny and take off down the road at full speed. Then she would stop and be as still as if she did not want to move. Daddy would scold her and pull on the reins but it was difficult to keep the buggy on the road in one piece. He thought she was playing with him and being "ornery". After a while, daddy bought a bit and put it in her mouth. When she decided to stampede the bit would cut her mouth and make it bleed. After a few experiences with the bit Old Ed was cured. She learned to trot along and behave herself. When Old Ed ran away Poodle would do his best to keep behind the buggy. He always managed to be with it when it stopped. Old Jane was a quiet horse, not very strong but she would fall in with Old Ed for any caper. The third horse, Pet, was calm and did not cause trouble. Daddy worked her in the field. The fourth horse was a wild and mean buckskin pony with a nasty temper. She did something one day and daddy took a strap to her that she never forgot. When she was in the barn, he never entered her stall without calling her name and putting his hand on her hip. If he did not she would have kicked him to death. Not long after he had punished her he forgot to speak to her an she became enraged and started to pin him against the side of the stall. He was scared but looked up to see a pitchfork he had hung on the wall. He used all his might to reach it and stuck her with it. She never forgot and he never trusted her after that.

About 1907 a friend Ernest Page, who lived near the Crain's, wanted to take a trip to Florida. He had heard about people purchasing land in the Everglades, draining it, and selling it (the first Florida land boom). Perhaps Ernest just wanted a vacation from his family of four. Anyway, he asked daddy to go to Florida with him and daddy promised to go. Mother was disgusted as she wanted to go along too, but the two men decided to go alone, leaving their families behind.

Daddy asked his neighbor, Julius Brantz, an old time German bachelor friend to help with the chores. Julius had been a help to mother and she had baked light bread for him every week. He was always happy to come to our place to eat. He said when he came, "Hirnmel bread, she always smell so good."

He and mother got along well but a few days after daddy and Ernest had gone, mother had ear trouble which got worse and worse. At Dr. Tom's advice daddy was summoned home, much to his disgust. However, he came home with two napkin rings, a big pretty conchshell, a genuine alligator purse, a black ostrich feather fan for me, many pictures, and stories of the negroes, the ocean, and the history of early Florida. Mother got better but she lost the hearing in her right ear.

Daddy bought twenty acres of land in the Everglades and a lot in Fort Lauderdale. The land was on Lake Okeechobee. He kept this property and paid the taxes on it. He never forgot his trip to Florida and looking out over the ocean. Ernest Page didn't keep his land very long. Probably he neglected to pay the taxes on it.

I was not allowed to go to school because the nearest one in the county was about three miles from our home. Daddy said he did not want to take the time to take me and bring me home each day. There were no children near me to play with. Poodle became my only companion. I did not know how to play except with Poodle, a few wooden blocks, a small book made of cloth and the Montgomery Ward catalog. I could cut pictures out of the catalog and I loved that.

We did have the old wall telephone on a party line and a daily paper, the *Wichita Beacon*, which was always two days old when we received it. Our ring for the telephone was 2 longs and 3 shorts. When the phone rang the whole neighborhood listened in. When you took down the receiver you always heard the other receivers click. So if you did not want every one to know your business you did not mention it on the telephone. Sometimes in the morning when the men were out working, two old gossips would get on the line and were able to hear all the gossip for miles around. I was not allowed to use the phone and I could not reach it on the wall. "Central" was merely an older woman who spent 18 or 20 hours at the switchboard in Goltry and was subject to call during the night. Sometimes she would interrupt two people on the line in case of an accident or fire. Mother did not listen much because she was too busy.

About 1911 father became ill and did not have the strength to continue the backbreaking work on the homestead. I was still recovering from my bout with typhoid and mother wanted to be near her family in Missouri. It was decided to rent the homestead and look for a new home in Missouri. Daddy found a near–by poor family who would rent the place for a while. He sold his horses and hoped they would have good masters. Since Poodle was getting older and we were not sure of where we were going, and it would be difficult to uproot him, daddy left him with the new renters hoping he would be cared for.

Rumors had come to Goltry that there was a health spa at Claremore, Oklahoma. This health resort was on the same railroad we would use to travel to Missouri. Daddy decided to go to Claremore first and see if he could take the cure. We left the homestead in very early spring and spent about three months there.

Since we were living in the Cherokee Strip of the Indian Territory of Oklahoma you ask, "Why didn't you write about the Indians as well as the white settlers? The answer is simple: we never saw an Indian in that part of the strip although our county seat town was and still is named Cherokee. The Cherokee Indian Tribe was brought from Tennessee and Arkansas and forced to live on the reservation in the northeastern end of the strip some hundred miles from our homestead in the northwestern end. If you look on the map you will see that all the towns bearing Indian names like Muskogee, Pawhuskie, Sapulpa, and Tulsa are in the northeastern corner of Oklahoma. These are towns today with fewer whites than red men.

CLAREMORE

Claremore was an Indian town very close to Tulsa famous for its sulfur well and bath houses. It was the home of Will Rogers who was of Cherokee descent. We heard much of his early life and exploits but at the time we were there he was doing rope tricks on a New York stage for a living. We did not see him and at that time did not realize how well known he was.

Father rented a one room apartment in an "L" shaped 8 room one story rooming house about 2 blocks from the largest of the bath houses in downtown Claremore. The room contained a small kerosene three–burner cook stove, a table and three chairs, a shelf for dishes, pots, a dresser, a double bed and cot. I got the cot. The "L" shaped building had a porch running on the south and east sides. We had the west room at the end of the south porch. There were no bathrooms only an outhouse in the chicken yard surrounded by a high woven wire fence. I do not remember exactly what we paid for our living quarters but it was a small sum – about ten dollars a month. There was a board walk from the south porch and east porch around to the outhouse.

Going to the outhouse was my biggest problem and one that I have never forgotten. There was a mother and a small redheaded boy who lived in one of the last rooms on the east side. I do not remember the boy's name but he was about two years younger than I. In the afternoon when we came home from the bathhouse I had to go to the outhouse. The little boy watched. When I got inside and fastened the door, he decided he had to go too. He would come running and tell me to get out of there and if I did not he would scream and kick on the door until I did. I would be scared and would not come out so my mother had to knock on his mother's door and have her come to the rescue. The mother was not interested in her son's actions and I would sit there until someone came to my rescue. To this day I remember a little redheaded boy who tormented me.

Mother and I took the steam treatments in the bathhouse together. We would be placed on a wooden bench, naked, with a peak hole to hold our noses in, locked in for so many minutes. The steam was very strong. It was hard to breathe but we did sweat the poison out of our systems. Then we were toweled down, cooled off and given a little time to get our strength back before we walked home. Daddy had the same treatment in the men's department. Sometimes he was placed in a tent–like structure. The steam was released at the top of the tent. Some of the staff took a picture of him sitting in the tent with a towel covering his body and his head sticking out of the top of the tent. He paid for the picture and was quite proud of it until he came home and showed it to mother. Mother had a fit and he was not so proud. She was afraid one of her family would see the picture.

(How morals have changed since 1910!). We kept the picture for a long time but it disappeared after we came to Missouri.

Another part of the cure at Claremore was to drink the sulfur water (so much a day) and that nearly finished me. Daddy learned to drink the water by heating it. Mother was not so lucky and I never could get it down. Even the smell would gag me and I would throw up. One did not have to take a laxative either and that is why I hate little redheaded boys.

We did go to see the sulfur well while we were there. The well was never drilled or dug. The stream just came up out of the ground. The city government had it covered with a cement and wooden box and thought it would stop the flow of water. The flow was so powerful it wore holes in the six foot high box that allowed it to run off in a small stream into the river. It had been flowing for a few years when we saw it. The Indians did not seem to mind it but white people did not build homes on the windy side of it. When the wind blew we could not stand the odor. On one side there was a coating of yellow sulfur that smelled like rotten eggs. It stood out in a field by itself but the water was piped into the big bathhouses downtown and sometimes they had the distinctive odor of sulfur.

I saw the well in 1912 and again in 1982 when I went back to Claremore. I found that the well had dried up probably because of some change in the underground stream. One of the banks in Oklahoma covered the site of the well. I was in the city and that was the first thing I wanted to see. I inquired and was told that no one knew what it was but finally by talking to old timers they remembered the well and the bathhouses. At that time, 1910, Claremore, Oklahoma, was the spa of the western world, now completely forgotten. How times do change or are changed by Old Mother Nature. I did have the privilege in 1982 of seeing the famous Indian Mounds and grave sites on Claremore Hill. I remember as a child seeing the old Indian chiefs in their fancy dress standing by the side of the railroad station in Tulsa to review every train that passed through. They came every morning to see the trains and the whites who rode on them. After oil was found on their lands (the reservation) all one could see or hear was Indians and their automobiles.

In three months our family was better and we boarded the Tulsa train for a home in Missouri.

MISSOURI – THE GUYIOT PLACE

The Crain family arrived in Republic, Missouri, in May 1912 by way of the St. Louis and San Francisco Railroad Company (know as the "The Frisco") from Goltry and Claremore, Oklahoma. They were met at the railroad station by Hance Stalcup, husband of Minnie Owens Stalcup, mother's nearest sister in age and one who had worked in the fields with her to keep the family from starving. This couple had been married for several years and had four children. Uncle Hance had been adopted by Uncle Rance Blades when he was eleven years old. Uncle Hance and Aunt Minnie lived in North Republic in a five room house with two bedrooms. Because they were kind and helpful daddy did not feel he could impose on them and decided to rent the old Guyiot home on the north side of Uncle Rance's house. Uncle Rance and Aunt Kate owned forty acres of land between the Guyiot place and Uncle Hance so mother was nearby. The Guyiot's had rented their home and moved away. I believe it was to Iowa. They had placed their best furniture in a small room upstairs. The house had three rooms downstairs and two upstairs which mother loved. Because we had no furniture, dishes or anything to keep house with. We ate our meals at Uncle Rance's place. My father offered to pay Aunt Kate for our meals but she refused to accept any payment. Father bought a three–burner kerosene cook stove, a table and chairs, dishes, two chairs for the living room, two double beds, and some garden tools because there was a big garden area.

He also made me a rope swing. I had happy times playing in my swing on the limb of a peach tree on the north side by their bedroom. The swing was low as the limbs grew out about two feet above my head. I loved it. It was the first time I had ever seen a swing. Sunday morning I got up at 7 o'clock to go out and play in my swing. How surprised my parents were when they woke up and found me there. I remember going upstairs and playing on the floor in the vacant room. I cannot remember what I played with unless it was my ABC blocks and some little stones or some wild flowers that I had found in the back yard. I never had a doll. I was always obsessed with the locked door to the room with the furniture in it but I never went near it.

My father was first and always a farmer and so he hunted for odd jobs around the neighborhood working for farmers usually in their fields.

When September came school opened. I remember my first day of school. Mother had gone into town the day before and bought me a square tin lunch box and a green sack to hold my school supplies, a pencil box with a pencil, an eraser and a rough light brown pencil tablet to write on. There may have been other articles such as a small crayon box but I can't recall for sure.

We had to walk about three fourths of a mile through the main business street to school, a two story building of eight rooms and four basement rooms with a coal burning furnace in one end and the grade school rooms in which grades one through twelve were taught. I was curious and a little scared as mother found the first grade room with about thirty six and seven year olds in it. My mother told the teacher I had never been to school and that I knew nothing about reading and writing because we had lived in frontier Oklahoma and my father could not take time from farming to take me in his wagon three miles to school every day. The teacher wrote down my name and age in years only. Because it was the first of September and my birthday was the 18th she decided to call me eight years old when I was only seven. This got me into trouble sixty years later when I could not prove to the Social Security Authorities that I was sixty–five when my school record showed I was only sixty–four. I had to get my Oklahoma Census Record of 1910 which was a perfect proof of my age. My father had to work that day and did not go with us. He had decided that was mother's job. We had to walk because there was no other means of transportation. Mother left me in about an hour and I was to come back home with Aunt Minnie's oldest child Dessie, one month younger than I.

That first day of school we had to draw a picture and write our first name on it and hand it in. I raised my hand and said I did not know how to write my first name. My teacher walked over to the blackboard and wrote "Ada" on the board and I copied it. How thrilled I was to see my own first name on the board and be able to copy it for myself. The teacher seated me with another girl on the back seat in the room, probably because I was bigger than some of the other children. Two years can make a difference in size at that age.

Young people today would not understand that at recess time or any time we had to rise out of our seats we were required to march with our hands and arms stiffly hanging at our sides. We were not allowed to whisper and when recess ended we had to line up like little wooden soldiers according to grades one to twelve and march in single file again with not a whisper or even a smile. When we were excused most of the children had to march around my corner seat and it became a habit for each child to put his hand on my head as he marched around. It got to be a sport and my mother could not comb my hair because my head was sore, so she came to school to ask the teacher to move my seat.

About the middle of the term the teacher decided that because I was older I should be put in a more advanced section in the first grade. She moved me across the room and gave me an advanced first grade reader. I took one look at that book and I could not read one word and I could not ask my seat mate. I was scared and disoriented for about two weeks. I still remem-

ber the word "which" and how I struggled with
it but I did improve and was promoted to second grade at the end of the year. In second
grade I began to lead my class and had no further trouble.

THE NELSON HOUSE

In the late fall, on a bright sunny morning, my parents were talking in the kitchen. Father decided to open the south door onto the porch. He unknowingly walked over to the door and opened it to find Aunt Kate with her ear to the keyhole. She was surprised and quickly jumped back exclaiming, "I have decided to collect for your meals as I am in need of some ready cash." My father said, "I offered to pay you a month ago and you wouldn't accept any money." He became angry and refused to pay her. She was so taken by surprise that she did not know what to say. He decided he did not want any more eavesdropping and we moved to another place. He never trusted Aunt Kate after that.

We rented a small house in the north end of town which I will call the Nelson place. It was closer to school and I had to walk through an alley and into the baseball playground which I did not like because of the danger of being hit by baseballs. I remember two incidents. I was in second grade and when school closed my parents took me to the open house on the last night of school to see an Indian play call "Hiawatha" dramatized by the older students. During the night I woke up screaming, trying to climb the wall because the Indians were chasing me. My frightened parents called a doctor the next morning and I was diagnosed as having a bad case of German measles. However I recovered and enjoyed playing in the old barn on the Nelson property, under an old sycamore tree in the yard. I had never seen a sycamore tree before and the bark and large leaves intrigued me.

My father obtained work in the wheat harvest of a farmer north of town. One day a bad storm arose and mother and I took refuge in the middle of my bed. The wind blew very hard and we did not have screens on our windows. It hailed so hard with hailstones almost as big as baseballs. They broke our windows out and the water blew through the house. Everything was a mess. Mother was scared. The lightning and thunder were terrible. She was worried that my father was out in the storm and might have been hurt. However he came home and helped clean up the mess. The Nelson's had a cow and some chickens and an old–fashioned ice cream freezer at their home next door so they gathered up some of the hailstones and made ice cream. We were invited to share it. That is my first memory of eating ice cream and seeing it frozen. For some reason my father did not like renting from the Nelsons so we moved in a few months to a small house on Mill Street in South Republic called the Robertson place. Paved streets did not exist all over Republic but there were sidewalks and each lot was surrounded by a wire fence with a yard gate.

THE ROBERTSON HOUSE

We moved to the Robertson House on Mill Street in 1914 and I remember mother sending me to the grocery store one hot summer morning. I went barefoot. When I came back the sidewalk was so hot and I could not find any grass to walk on so I hurried as fast as I could but the soles of my feet got burned. I have two specific memories with this house also. I had an illness called Roseola and one wet fall evening my father took me for a walk. He did not talk very much but was concerned that I was able to walk. It had been misty and the whole world seemed to be covered with dewdrops. There was the most beautiful red sunset that evening. At that house was a homemade wooden doll cradle that I played with and when we moved away I wanted to take the doll cradle with me but daddy said, "No, it isn't ours and we must leave it here." My heart was broken but we moved without it.

My mother had to go out in the country to care for her sister who was having a baby. She tried to leave us with enough light bread until she got back but she did not get back until the light bread had molded. This can happen in a day or two without refrigeration. I did not know how to cook but my father thought I should. He did not have much patience with me. Mother came home and I did not feel happy with my Aunt because she was always having babies and she always had to call my mother. She had twelve children and I hated her for years because I was always left alone to do the housework and cooking.

I have memories of playing beside a bush in our front yard called the Rose of Sharon. Another memory is somewhat unpleasant and that is being afraid of our neighbor's two Doberman Pinscher dogs which to me were as big as horses and had nasty tempers.

While we lived in the Robertson house mother used to make fancy dresses for many ladies as she was a good seamstress. I got used to their coming and going for fittings.

The small son of the Robertsons became very ill when we lived here and one night mother took care of him. She bathed him with whiskey to bring his fever down and it worked. The next morning the parents wanted to know what mother did to him but she knew they were opposed to whiskey and wouldn't tell. His family tried for years to find out what she had done but she was always afraid to tell them.

FIVE ACRE TRACT

Father decided to buy a piece of land that was called the "Five Acre Tract". It was east of Republic almost a mile from school. My happiest days were spent here. One acre of the five was composed of old apple trees. In the spring I used to climb each tree to find the robins' nests. I guess the robins did not like it as they protested when I walked down the row of trees. I never molested their nests but looked in to see how many eggs were there.

We lived at that place from 1915 until 1919. I had a long walk, almost a mile to school. The walk was unusual. When I left school I walked northeast along a village street past the stately house of Walter A. Coon, the town banker. I wished I could go inside but I was never able to. I watched it burn down one night years later.

On the other side of the street was the "Frisco" Railroad tracks and the red brown depot. I crossed Main Street with business buildings on each side and the main railroad crossing with posts and a large hook on each side of the crossing in which were hung the mail pouches for fast passenger trains to pickup during the night. The railroad tracks here were built up on one side to an embankment. I would cross the main street and walk along the embankment about a block to the section house where my cousin Clara lived when Uncle Spud worked in the Republic Section. Uncle Spud's family came back from Oklahoma a few months after we left and he started work in the Republic Section. Afterwards he became Section Foreman at Billings. I climbed the bank by the tool house, crossed the main track and four switch tracks into the Big Mill and Lumber Coal Companies' loading stations. It was not a good way but I could cut off about two blocks. Along the bank from the main crossing to the section house were weeds (Spanish Needles) also huge chunks of coal and some gravel. I was frightened until I got across the tracks. Mother caused my fright because she sent me off in the mornings with this warning, "Now you watch that railroad track so you won't get hurt." Once my father and I got caught between two moving freight trains going in opposite directions and we walked to the crossing before one freight train passed on. How frightened I was. I suspect my father was frightened too but he never showed it. He cautioned me never to let that happen again. My head swam and I could not keep an equal distance between the two moving trains. They were moving fast and the incident lasted only a few moments. We had decided when we first got on the tracks that we could walk to the crossing alongside the one train but the other came in quickly beside us. We never tried that again.

When I crossed the tracks I came to the end of Pine Street and walked a cinder path about a block. In the middle of Pine Street there was a huge old elm tree, about 70 years old and the biggest elm I have ever seen. From the elm was a dirt road with houses on the north side, then a turn north in the road for about a block, then a turn east where there were houses. A block east the road sloped down to a ravine. On the north side of this road was a meadow with a windmill and a trough for watering stock. The windmill and well were used for water for spraying commercial apple orchards. On the north side of the meadow were the Robertson Apple Orchards with huge old Ben Davis apple trees, some more than forty feet tall. It had been a huge orchard but when we moved there only about ten acres were left.

I climbed the little hill. The road ran between the Roy Jackson Orchard on the north side and the J. R. Derry Orchard on the south side. The J. R. Derry Orchard was a young one and most of the trees were beginning to bear fruit. The Jackson Orchard was a little older. Both were ten acres in size and in the spring the trees in bloom were a delight. If it was late in the afternoon, I felt afraid that I might encounter a stranger or a tramp running out into the road. I would hold my breath after I had passed a person on that part of the road.

My father had worked in both orchards and that was where he got the idea of buying the Five Acre Tract because it bordered on the east side of the Jackson Orchard. The one acre of apple trees on it was an extension of the Jackson Orchard.

You could almost tell the month of the year by the smells that came out of those two orchards. In the spring the apple blossom, in the summer the sprays on the trees, in the fall the decaying apples on the ground, the picking crews in the winter, the snow and cold north wind blowing through the trees. When my family moved to the Five Acre Tract I was in school and I will always remember my first afternoon walk to my new home. It was late in the fall and the apples had been picked but a few rotten ones remained on the ground under the trees. When I reached home there was the same smell of rotten apples in our back yard. When my father bought the place, the first thing that he did was have the place surveyed so he could build a fence around it. That fence had to be woven wire about five feet high with barbed wire on top to keep out animals and people. It was difficult to climb a woven wire fence and you could easily tear the seat of your pants on the top barbed wire. Most people did not try it so we felt protected. The iron gates were strong with woven wire on them. Father always kept the fences in good repair and woe to anyone who interfered with them.

THE FIVE ACRE TRACT – VYDETH AND CLARA

The Five Acre Tract opened up a whole new world for me. It was a new way of life. The apples were Ben Davis or York Imperial but I found one lone Winesap tree. It was a replant and had just begun to bear when we moved there. I liked the apples on that tree because they were hard, sour and ripened very late so my father said that tree in our orchard was my very own. There were two things I loved to do, read and sew for my dolls. One summer I earned several dollars picking strawberries and the first thing I did was buy two dolls, a blond and a black hair one at the drug store. Their bodies were stuffed with saw dust and they had china heads, hands, and feet. I did not play with them as much as I made clothes for them, cutting my own patterns and sewing the clothes by hand. My cousin, Clara, and I loved to play house outdoors with them and we dressed them up for weddings and parties. One night after school I stopped at Clara's home at the Section House because she was going to spend the night with me and we would go to school together the next morning since we were both in the same room at school but in different grades. At this time Clara was about eleven and in the fifth grade and I was thirteen and in the sixth grade. After school we hurried to the Section House for

Clara to get her night clothes. As we were nearing the Section House Clara whispered to me that she hoped her sister Vydeth would be asleep and would not hear us come in. As soon as we entered the door Vydeth heard us and came out of her room and wanted to hear everything that was said. Aunt Cora sent Clara in to get her sleeping clothes and of course Vydeth wanted to know what was happening so Aunt Clara had to tell her. She began to beg to go too and Aunt Cora said , "No, you will have to walk at least a half a mile and the girls can't carry you." Vydeth began to cry and thus started the story Clara and I had to listen to until we were both grown. "I want to go too. I never get to go any place. Clara and Ada go to school and play together all the time but I never get to do anything." Aunt Cora tried to explain to her that it was fall and cold weather and that Clara and Ada could not carry her. Then she said, "You aren't used to being away from home at night and Aunt Maud and Uncle Ern can't take care of you. When it gets night you will be afraid and they can't bring you home." But she wouldn't listen to any arguments saying, "I won't cry and I can walk. I promise I will walk every step of the way." Finally Aunt Cora gave in and let her go.

Clara was dismayed but I was not too upset. Guess I did not know little kids very well.

We started down the cinder path to the big elm and of course she was entranced by everything she saw on the way. Without coaxing she walked all the way.

When we got home mamma and daddy were surprised but they accepted the situation. Poor Clara was about to cry. She knew she could not play with me but would have to tend to Vydeth's wants and needs. Mother got supper for us. She brought out a loaf of hot light bread which Clara loved and she felt better. Daddy held Vydeth on his lap and tried to entertain her most of the evening. I was surprised.

We got up early the next morning and got Vydeth ready. She was tired and sleepy but we had to start early so we would not be late for school. Daddy had to work in the apple orchard so he could not go with us.

It was a cold and damp morning with the wind blowing from the north. We were alright as long as we were going through the orchards but when we got to the open places Vydeth began to get cold, her feet became very cold, her nose became red and she began to cry. I was older by two years so I picked her up and tried to carry her, then Clara tried but she was too heavy for us. We struggled and in turn carried her a short distance. We reached the Section House worn out with a whimpering Vydeth and late for school. Aunt Cora saw us and walked across the tracks to meet us. She was so glad to get Vydeth back home in one piece she forgot to scold any of us. We were late for school and in those days being late for school was a cardinal sin. Our teacher in that room lived on the cinder path street that we walked down but that did not help much as she rode to school.

"OLD RED"

When we had lived at the "Five Acre Tract" for a short time, my grandfather who owed mother a debt brought us a red milk cow whom we called "Old Red". She was a contrary, self–willed creature but she did give rich milk so we had milk and butter. Daddy nearly always kept Old Red in her stall in the barn at night especially if it was cold.

One of our neighbors had an mother cat that she did not want and knowing my love for cats she gave it to me, much to my parents' disgust. The old cat had five kittens and I ended up having to put the five kittens each in a small crate at night to keep an old male cat from killing them. He did carry two away, one came back and I had to give the others away.

Late in the fall, about Christmas time, I put the cat in the barn to keep her warm. The hayloft was filled to the top with bales of straw and the lower half except Old Red's stall was layered with apple barrels full of apples which we kept for our own winter use. That night before daylight we awoke to a terrible noise. We could hear Old Red squealing and kicking the side of the barn. My father got up, put on his clothes and coat and went out to the barn to see what the trouble was. When he opened the door to her stall he found the cat hanging on Old Red's back for dear life. Old Red was trying to shake her off. The boards in the corner of the barn were broken and hanging. Daddy did not go close for fear of getting kicked but he got the pitchfork and pointed it at her along with trying to pull a spitting and scared cat off her back. The only thing we could think was that the cat was looking for a warm place to sleep and had climbed up the side of Old Red's stall and feeling the warmth from her body, had leaped on her back and started to knead her with her paws. When Old Red felt her paws she grew angry, could not dislodge her, started kicking, and went berserk. The cat was not about to give up a warm place. I had to find a home for the cat and daddy had to rebuild the corner of the barn.

I loved to dress up my dolls. So one bright morning in the spring I went out to the new apple house, got a shoe box and proceeded to line the shoe box for a coffin, then went to get the spade to dig a hole by the door to bury my dead. I left my dolls buried for about a week and decided to dig them up and see how well they had slept. They were all right so I reburied them and left them for about a week again. At the end of the week my father came in the house and said that he had learned that we were going to have a big rain storm so I hurried out and dug them up. I do not know whether he knew what I had done but mother did. Maybe she had told him and they were waiting to see what I would do. I know she kept telling me if it rained I would ruin my dolls and have an awful mess. However it did not rain for two weeks after I panicked and dug them up.

The Carter family in front of their barn near Angola, Indiana before starting their journey to Oklahoma in 1878

The farm home of Ernest Crain's uncle near Angola, Indiana

The author at five years of age in Jet, Oklahoma

Ready for her first day in school is eight year old Ada Crain

Maudie Owens Crain at 16 years of age

The author graduates from Springfield, Missouri State
Teachers College in 1924

The Congregational parsonage on North Main Street in
Republic, Missouri

Ernest and Maudie Crain in 1948

Ernest Crain's sister Edith and husband Otis

The author in 1977

PLANTING CORN

One spring Saturday morning my father announced at the breakfast table that he wanted to plant an acre of corn to feed Old Red for the next year and he did not think that he could do it by himself. I do not know whether he planned to teach me to work as well as play or whether he really needed some help. He had hired a man to plow and harrow the field the day before. I wonder if he was wishing he had had a son instead of daughter to help him on the farm. I was supposed to go with him to the field and drop the seed. The rows had been laid off and I was to go along ahead of him and put two kernels in the row about two feet apart. He would follow and cover them with the hoe. I tried but I could not measure each hill two feet apart so he became annoyed with me and finally went to an apple tree to cut a twig as long as he wanted and made me a measure for each hill. The hills were to match the other rows exactly so that they were all planted in a square. We worked all day in the hot sun until I got so tired I felt I would drop. He kept cautioning me to be exact but otherwise he did not talk much to me. He was farmer enough to want a perfect checkerboard in his corn field. I tried but I could care less whether corn was planted in a checkerboard pattern or not. He was a perfectionist and never asked me to help him plant corn again.

OSAGE ORANGE TREES

Some Missouri apple orchards and fields were surrounded by Osage orange hedges instead of fences. An Osage hedge served as a windbreak on the north side of a field or orchard and made a good substitute for a fence. An old healthy one might grow some fifteen feet high and its trunks and branches would spread and intertwine with each other. The trees had huge thorns from the ground to the top and these would grow four inches long and be as big around as a lead pencil. Livestock would steer clear of them and people would not break through. Our pasture and Roy Jackson's orchard had them on the north side half way between country roads.

My father had built a fence from the hedge south between our orchard and barn and Roy's apple orchard so that fence ran down the middle between two rows of apple trees. The fence was about five feet high, of woven wire and had barbed wire on top so you did not care to climb it. He extended this type of fence along the north side of the place about four feet beyond the Osage orange hedge so that if you got over the fence safely you could go no farther. Thieves got the idea of breaking into a storage house and stealing apples after the picking season was over. Our orchard was too small for a storage house so father stored the apples in the barn and locked the big double doors. The barn was not built like most barns in those days but was a long tall shed with double doors at one end and with a side door at the back of the first stall. He stored about twenty barrels and twenty big baskets of choice apples, MacIntosh and York Imperials, in the end where the double doors were and kept that part locked with a padlock day and night. Because of the apples he did not have much room for hay but he could sell the apples about Christmas time to nearby neighbors and farmers who came with a team and wagon to pick them up. For some reason a hole appeared in the Osage orange hedge at the corner of Roy's orchard and thieves got the idea of driving a small truck through the north pasture, taking a wheelbarrow through a row of apple trees, climbing the barbed wire fence, breaking the lock on the double doors and helping themselves to a basket of apples. How they lifted a huge basket of apples over the fence I will never know but we lost our apple baskets in spite of the barbed wire and hedge.

MARTHA AND DISOBEDIENCE

One summer afternoon in August I asked my parents if I could visit my friend Martha Montgomery. My parents said that I might go but I was to stay only until 4:30 P.M. I had to walk north through the Jackson Orchard, through a forty acre corn field, down a country road, cross the railroad tracks, down another long country road and up a hill to her home. It was so hot and I had not seen the corn field before so I fearfully walked along the fence and remembered my mother's usual admonish, "You watch that railroad track and crossing."

Martha took me out to her playhouse and showed me all her playthings and then out to their watermelon patch. Her mother had cut a big watermelon and had it cooling in the shade in a tub of cold water from the well. We enjoyed the watermelon and homemade cookies and I asked to go in the house to look at the clock. It was 4:30 and I said I must go home but Martha persuaded me that it was too hot and my father would not care if I stayed an hour longer. We were playing out in the front yard when I suddenly looked up and saw my father walking down the road toward the house. We went to the edge of the yard to meet him.

He said, "Didn't I tell you to start for home at 4:30 and it's now after 5:00?"

I was scared but Martha said, "Please, I didn't mean to get her in trouble and I persuaded her to stay." Her mother agreed.

He said, "You go get your bonnet and we will be on our way." I did and we started on our way. I tried to tell him I did not think it was wrong to stay a little longer but he did not say very much and I walked along beside him feeling guilty and yet not realizing what he had in mind.

When we got home, I went in the kitchen telling my mother what a good time I had had and he went to the woodshed. Then he came back to the back porch with a lathe. When I saw the lathe I realized what was going to happen to me. He called me out of the kitchen and gave me the hardest whipping I had ever had and never said a word. The lathe cut across my shoulders and really hurt but I guess I was scared as much as I was hurt. I cried to my mother and she said, "I am sorry but he told you to come home at 4:30 and I can't say a word so you will just have to take your medicine." We ate supper together and he did not say another word to me all evening. I was fourteen years old and that was the last whipping he ever gave me but I have never forgotten it. I tried to obey him always after that.

A RED COAT AND A FLOWER GARDEN

My father would never allow my mother or me to wear anything red because that was the color immoral women wore.

One fall I needed a new coat to wear to school and church so on Saturday morning father took me to town to the R. E. Thurman Dry Goods Store. Uncle Bob Thurman had several coats that I could wear, one of which was red with a square black velvet collar. I liked it but I did not say I did because it was red. Uncle Bob must have sensed I like it and he had it on sale so he "bragged it up" saying it was the prettiest, cheapest, and best made coat he had in the store. Daddy bought the coat. I went home happy with a new coat and told my mother how surprised I was. She was surprised too. He bought our clothes in brown because he liked it. Oh, how my mother and I hated brown! I wore the coat many times and he did not seem to notice that it was red.

I wanted a flower garden so we bought some old fashioned petunia seeds and I planted them in the garden beside the fence. They grew well and so did the weeds. I was so proud of them but I could not take time to keep them weeded. One fall evening he told me that I needed to weed them. I decided I would have to pull the weeds so I came home from school the next afternoon and he reminded me that he was going to weed the garden the next day. I did not pay much attention and the next afternoon I came home from school and decided to go out and admire my flowers. When I got to the garden, no weeds, no flowers. At the supper table I cried and said, "Why are my petunias gone?" He looked at me and said, "I was pulling weeds and there were more weeds than petunias so I didn't take time to look for petunias. If you want to have flowers you must keep the weeds out of them." He did not have any patience with weeds in a garden. In after years he often weeded the garden to have something to do.

POODLE

My next little picture concerns my pet dog Poodle. When we decided to leave Oklahoma, daddy rented the homestead to an acquaintance who needed the place and because we did not think we could bring Poodle to Missouri and were not sure where we would live daddy asked our renter if he would keep Poodle on the farm. It was difficult to go off and leave Poodle with a strange family but we risked it.

When we lived on the "Five Acre Tract" in Republic, Missouri, daddy had to go back to the homestead to look after the place and to repair fences. When he came home he said that he did not feel that the homestead was being cared for properly like an owner would and that Poodle did not look as if he had been cared for either. He knew the dog was unhappy. In a few months our caretaker wrote that he was buying another farm and daddy would have to get another renter.

There was a time just before World War I in which western farmers could get a dollar a bushel for corn. They began plowing up pasture lands, selling off their cattle and putting every foot of land into cultivation. Daddy had a chance to sell his homestead but what to do with Poodle who was still alive but getting old. He decided to have the renter put Poodle in a crate with food and water and send him on the railroad train to Missouri rather than put him to death. Besides, I had begun to cry and ask for Poodle. That did it.

Poodle was put in a crate and not too big a one at that. The crate was put in a baggage car on the Frisco Railroad and shipped to Missouri. I am glad I was not there when he was placed on the train. It took more than one man to do it. I suspect he was given a shot before they succeeded. We had a rural telephone at home and one evening after the evening passenger train arrived the local agent called us and told us he had a dog in a crate and urged us to come at once. The agent was upset and scared so we walked as quickly as we could to the express office. By that time it had taken 2 or 3 more men to get the crate out of the baggage car and into the freight office. The agent was shaken. He told my father he would not go near that crate let alone open it up. My father was not bothered and my mother said, "He won't hurt me." So she went up to the crate and daddy took a hammer and loosened one of two boards. Poodle bared his teeth and growled. Mother went up to the crate and put her hand on Poodle's head and said, "Hello Puppets." The mouth closed, the growls ceased. She rubbed his head a little and the other planks were loosened. By that time the agent had immediate business in his office. I stood a little way off and gazed at Poodle. Mother kept coaxing and finally Poodle could get up on numb and weak legs and step out of that crate. Mother got him outdoors where he could relieve himself. After two days it must have been a great relief. She had brought some food and water along with her and she fed him a few mouthfuls. He looked up at her and ate a little at a time.

When daddy had settled the bill, mother said, "Come on, Whippets, let's go home." She reached out her hand and Poo just looked at her and tried to follow her out of the station with daddy and I following behind. I wonder now how the poor creature could walk almost a mile but when he seemed to lag behind mother would coax and pat his head and he would try to switch his tail and follow. He did not seem to know daddy or I were around.

When we got him home he followed us into the house and laid down to rest. I remember talking to him and petting him and he seemed to like it. That night he slept on the floor by mother's side of the bed and never made a noise.

I knew he loved fried potatoes. When I came home from school and we had supper I would give him a whiff of the potatoes and he would follow me in hot pursuit. I would let him enjoy his supper of warm fried potatoes. What were his dog thoughts of what had happened to him in those two days? He lived in peace and quiet with us for nearly two years after that.

One day mother said, "Poodle is sick out in the old chicken house and I don't think he will recover." She and I went out and he was lying on his side but he did not seem to know we were there. The next morning he was still lying on his side dead. Daddy dug a grave for him in the northeast corner of our pasture between the barbed wire fence and Osage orange hedge. Daddy said he chose that spot because he thought that no wild animal would dare face the thorns and barbed wire to dig up his remains.

Poodle lived to be more than 13 years old. I never saw the poor dog's grave because I had to walk such a long distance between the barbed wire fence and Osage orange thorns. We all cried at his death thinking what a beautiful animal he had been and what a friend he had been to me. How he had saved me more than once from the Oklahoma rattlesnakes. He was the only playmate I had until I was eight years old and yet he remembered my mother the most because she fed him and cared for him when he was hurting.

ILLNESS

While we were living on the "Five Acre Tract", daddy became ill. He had a sick stomach, lost weight and strength. I do not know that I ever heard the doctor say what the illness was but he was in bed for almost two weeks. I do remember that Dr. O. N. Carter said that he smoked too many cigars, "stogies", he called them and if he did not stop it he would not live. After that if he even smelled tobacco smoke he would feel deathly ill. We always thought the doctor gave him something that turned him against tobacco. Doctor would never say of course. Gradually he got over the illness and he carried his corn cob pipe in his pocket but never used it. He became so happy over the situation that he bragged about it but he began to be addicted to chewing gum and mother and I wished he would make himself sick over gum, but no such luck.

After we left this home we had a clock shelf hanging high upon the wall of our kitchen. Father always put his dentures in a glass on the shelf beside the clock and his cud beside it. Sometimes he had several cud on the shelf and we used to get so disgusted at him about it but we kept still. We said we did not know which was the worst, pipe smoking or gum chewing. He never did smoke after that and it probably lengthened his life.

Daddy was patriotic while we were living on "The Five Acre Tract." World War I broke out and he thought he ought to do his part so he went to the draft board and offered his services. They would not accept him because he was too old. He was disappointed but he did his bit at home. He attended all the rallies and decided to support the war effort too. Whenever I brought home a report card with all A's on it I received a Baby Bond. Of course I did not object to that. Daddy did not feel well so he decided to sell our home. He said, "Maybe we won't have so much work to do or so far to walk to church if we bought another place in downtown Republic." He began to look around for a place to buy. He sold the "Five Acre Tract" to a family my mother had known for many years. There were four children in that family ranging in age from 5 to 14. How they managed to live in that small house I will never know.

THE WEIDNER PLACE

He found a new place to buy, a brick house with eight rooms on aristocratic Pine Street about a block from the Christian Church that we attended. It had a yard with flowering plants, two trumpet vines and roses beside a small barn and fertile garden.

Mother and I loved the place but we could not move in at once and we were disappointed. We had to wait for possession so we moved Old Red and our farm tools into the barn. The family that lived there had never used the barn. No one wanted to rent us a house for only a month so we had a problem. Finally my mother's father said that we could move our furniture into his house and stay with him for a month. After my grandparents' divorce my grandfather sold his forty acres, worked at picking apples in the Republic Orchards, rented a room over one of the stores on Main Street and finally bought the Weidner Place next door to Aunt Minnie and Uncle Hance where we first landed after coming from Oklahoma. This was March of 1919 and since we had no other place to go for a month my father reluctantly consented. Mother was apprehensive because she knew that there was no love lost between my father and grandfather and she was not sure if it would work out. We used my Uncle Hance's farm wagon and team to move our furniture and personal possessions to the Weidner Place.

I escaped the disorder in the daytime because I had to go to school but at night I would come to a house that had furniture and wooden boxes piled in each room. We did not unpack and tried to use just what we had to, but one never knew where things were or whether they were ours or grandfather's. I give both men credit for getting along well—a thing that had never happened before.

The saddest thing about our sojourn at the Weidner Place was my Uncle Hance's illness. Uncle Hance was a likable man whom we all loved. He farmed for a living as much as he could. He had to give that up and started to haul supplies from Springfield to the grocery and feed stores in Republic with his wagon and team. It was not an easy job on roads not blacktop and he had to give that up. He was never a strong man. He suffered from asthma, heart trouble and finally pneumonia about the time we moved there.

I remember one Saturday morning he grew worse and Aunt Minnie called Dr. Carter. Daddy, mother and I were standing on their porch near his room when the doctor came out. Aunt Minnie had raised him up in bed so that he could breathe better and mother had taken one year old Dolly in to see her father when the doctor came out. Mother hurriedly brought Dolly out in the porch where the rest of us were standing.

You could hear Uncle Hance gasping for breath. When the doctor entered the room Uncle Hance tried to smile between gasps and said, "How much longer will it be?"

Dr. Carter replied after feeling his pulse, "Not much longer Hance." Uncle Hance made two or three gasps after that and was gone. We were all weeping except Dolly for she was too young to understand. There is a moment in our lives we never forget. My father liked Uncle Hance very much and he was especially kind to Dolly in later years.

THE BRICK HOUSE

Finally time passed and we could move into our new home. How happy we were! Every room had to be scrubbed from ceiling and woodwork to floors. Even daddy had to help. Mother made white curtains to hang in the window. There were fourteen long windows, four glass doors and ten foot ceilings. Mother and daddy chose the big front bedroom downstairs and gave me my choice of the three bedrooms upstairs. My choice was the front one. I was thrilled. It had a small clothes closet, a front window and one window on the side. Being upstairs alone did not bother me a bit. It was the first room of my own. When winter came it was cold (no heat except a stove downstairs in the kitchen and one in the living room) so I had to move downstairs into a bedroom so small that I had room only for my bed and the ironing board. That I did not like but I survived.

Something happened to Old Red. She could not have any more calves so no butter and milk and we had to sell her. However, we did have the nicest garden we ever had in Republic.

While we lived in the brick house someone gave me a kitten. I loved it so much and took it every place I went. I knew daddy did not want me to have the kitten because I was not well and he thought I should not be around a pet too much. That summer I had had a bad case of

malaria with severe bouts of chills and high fever. Where I got it I do not know except that we
did have mosquitoes. One afternoon I was in
the kitchen with my kitten and it ran under
daddy's feet and he crushed it. He was crabby.
The kitten died the next day and he said that I
ought not to have any more kittens if I did not
take care of them. I cried but he did not seem to
have sympathy for me. I never did forgive him
for it and he seemed to hate animals after that.

We had a neighbor, Jim Cox, who became
friendly with my father. He was an unusual
character inclined to brag about his possessions
of which he had a brand new car (very costly)
and a nice house and lot. I do not know whether
he became jealous of daddy and our family.
Daddy did not like him and one day in the
summer he told my dad that he had been talking with the men who had built our house and
that one of them had said that the bricks in the
house were laid with lime mortar and the house
would not stand after several years. Every
week or so he told my father that he had better
get rid of the place before it fell down. The
house was beginning to get old when we bought
it so my father started to worry about it thinking he had a lemon on his hands. Daddy became discouraged and worried. My mother
could not do much about it so she began to
think she might have to move again.

By this time we had a new doctor in town
whose name was Pierce and one day he appeared on the scene and wanted to buy our
home. We had engaged him as our doctor since

our favorite doctor had died soon after we moved. Dr. Pierce offered daddy a good price for the brick house and daddy was relieved and decided to sell. My mother was devastated. She cried and told daddy she would not sign the deed and that made him angry. For a week or two we did not have a happy home. Dr. and Mrs. Pierce came two or three times and told us they would take out the center portion downstairs in the living room and build a fireplace. My mother loved a fireplace and she resented Dr. Pierce so I cried too. Mother gave in and said she would sign the deed. There was nothing else she could do without breaking up her home. She did not feel very kindly toward Jim Cox the rest of her life. Daddy had given me two little rosebushes which I set out in the front yard. I asked him if I might ask Dr. Pierce to dig them up so I could take them but he said, "No, they were on the property and a part of the deal." That rankled me for a long time but daddy never realized what he had done. So the brick house became the property of Dr. Pierce and his wife with mother and me shedding bitter tears but daddy feeling relieved. Jim Cox and Dr. Pierce both lived less than five years after we moved.

I do not know whether Jim Cox and Dr. Pierce were working against us or not. I still love that place and many years afterward whenever I went home from Michigan I would walk around that house and look at it. This happened in 1919 and that place has changed hands several times but the walls are still standing as strong as ever even though the bricks were put together with lime mortar.

THE CONGREGATIONAL PARSONAGE

Daddy found that the Congregational Parsonage on Main Street, a block from us, was for sale and he could make some money on the deal. He did not have any trouble. The Congregational Church and Parsonage by its side were deteriorating. The congregation had moved away and died off until only two or three members were left in Republic. The windows were broken out of the church, the steeple and front entrance were in ruins, but the parsonage was in good condition, rented and occupied but a frame house and a much smaller one of five rooms. Dr. Pierce was an impatient man who wanted immediate possession and he got it but the next week when daddy wanted immediate possession of the parsonage he did not get it. He had to abide by the law and wait a month. There we were without a home again after only one year.

There was an empty house of four rooms on the north side of the Christian church where we attended about four houses down from our new home so the Crain family had to move out bag and baggage into this empty house. It was the second time in a year that we moved and found ourselves stumbling over boxes and furniture in a new home. We did not unpack except what we needed to eat, wear and sleep in. All of us were weary and heartsick. Finally the month passed and we moved into our "new" and last residence in Republic. The house needed paint on the outside and a new porch at the back. There was a long row of huge black walnut trees along the south side of the lot. A storm had come through the year before and most of the trees had fallen. They were still bearing leaves and walnuts.

Daddy did two things at once, cut the trees down and built a woven wire fence with barbed wire on top around the entire lot. The trees were dying and not very good to sell for lumber so he cut them for firewood. In those days walnut lumber was not worth much on the market. The next thing he did was to have the lot surveyed and found that it extended over about a foot into the neighbor's driveway. There was a curb on the other side of the neighbor's driveway so when daddy got the fence built it was difficult for the neighbor to use his driveway without running into the fences on our side or the curb on his side. There was trouble for a while but my dad could be stubborn when it was his property. Finally, the neighbor had to set his curb over.

School began the last of August and it was my first year of high school. High school children had the same building that I had had in the first grade. The high school section occupied half of the upper story and we were crowded. Whenever we had assembly we had to open big sliding doors. There were some small rooms in the basement and the juniors and seniors used them. We were so crowded that an election had been held and a new high school was being built about a block east of our home.

We moved into the new high school after Christmas in 1920. In our eyes that was a big event. The school was modern and spacious for those times and we were proud of it.

A week or two before the new high school opened a smallpox epidemic broke out and we had to go to the high school to be vaccinated. Mother would not take the vaccination. She had had one when vaccinations were new and her arm became so sore that her mother had put a poultice on it. Of course that was the wrong thing to do and she almost lost her arm so she said she would rather have smallpox than another infected arm. Daddy and I went, enjoyed seeing the new building and were vaccinated. My arm did not bother me but my father had a headache and fever for two or three days.

I went to school in the new building and could come home for lunch which we enjoyed as a family. Mother had a hot lunch ready and I looked forward to that and was always hungry when I came home. We had our main meal at noon and left the leftovers for a meal at night. Daddy liked that but he expected to sit down at the stroke of twelve or five. Mother was expected to be there ready with the meal.

One day after we moved there was a knock at the door and mother found Uncle Worth Crain, my father's youngest brother at the door. He had visited us once before when we lived at the Nelson place and he had taken a notion to come to Missouri.

He was daddy's youngest brother and had a cobbler's shop in Jet, Oklahoma. As a child, before the family came to Indiana, he had had a serious illness, a fever and it affected his brain but he could live by himself and earn a living. He seemed to have lots of friends in Jet. Uncle Worth liked to play the violin and sing old–time songs. This time he brought a second violin, a very old one that he had taken the varnish off to improve the sound. He gave the violin to me. I knew absolutely nothing about music. A piano teacher living near us offered to give me music lessons but daddy said, "No, I was like him. I couldn't even carry a tune," and he did not have the money to spend for no results. So I never had a chance to learn. To this day I cannot sing or read music. After Uncle Worth was gone, he gave the violin to a man who said he could re-varnish it and use it.

Uncle Worth always came with a suitcase full of dirty clothes and mother always went out of her way to wash and mend them and cook all the foods she knew he liked. He never stayed more than a week and daddy always seemed glad when he was gone. He did not have much patience with Uncle Worth because he was not a farmer. Uncle Worth earned his way, lived alone and loved people even if he was not very bright. I never saw him again.

MAKING A NEW HOME

When we moved to the parsonage it had four rooms: a pantry downstairs and one big room upstairs with three small windows. At the back of the house was a small wooden porch which daddy decided to enclose and put windows on the south side. We used this porch for our kitchen which worked out very well. There was no room for a cook stove so we cooked on a three burner kerosene stove with a small portable oven on the top. We had a small metal table and cupboard. In the dining room we kept our old cook stove, table, cabinet, and dish cupboard. There was also a 2 x 4 x 1 sink with a pitcher pump connected by pipes to a huge cistern. We did not drink the cistern water because it was not correctly filtered but our little city voted for and established a public water system. That made us happy. Daddy decided he had enough money to redo the huge pantry room and make a modern bathroom with a stool and an old–fashioned bathtub set on claws. For hot water we had a kerosene water heater that worked much like our modern gas water heaters. The lavatory was small but like ours of today. Each one had his own towel and wash cloth. In order to have a bathroom we had to have a cesspool for sewage disposal so daddy consulted a friend of his who was a contractor and the cesspool was built according to government regulations. It was big enough to take care of the waste water for two or three homes. How we loved that bathroom. It was the first one on our street for two or three blocks. Soon bathrooms were the style in Republic.

Mother and I had mourned leaving the brick house but God made up for our disappointment by giving us a bathroom.

Daddy built a washhouse for mother. In these women boiled their white clothes in a wash boiler on a stove or in a big black iron kettle outside. Mother thought her clothes were not clean unless they were boiled, rinsed twice, blued and then hung on an outside clothes line to dry. We had a flat topsy stove in the new washhouse, a bench for two big washtubs with a hand wringer and a washboard. Later we were able to find a hand propelled washing machine. The family wash had to be done on Monday and hung out to dry to vie with the neighbor ladies to see who could hang their clothes on the line first. Tuesday was ironing day, Wednesday was mending. Thursday and Saturday were baking days, and Friday was shopping day. In addition, daddy built another part to the washhouse, a garage. He said that maybe he would buy a car sometime or that the place would sell better if there was a garage. However the style of cars had changed from the old fashioned "Tin Lizzie" so the garage was not long enough to hold the new cars. Daddy never bought a car and used the garage for a storage house. The real reason was that he had always driven horses and he did not think he could ever learn to drive a car. He was not mechanically inclined either. Since we never had a car, I did not come near a car and I never learned to drive; too much like my father. I have regretted that I did not learn to drive a car and now I am too old.

Some years after we bought the parsonage, the Congregational Church next door was torn down. Joe McMillan, a Missouri State Representative who lived in Republic, bought the lot and lumber, built a house next to us on the north side and lived there for several years.

We were glad to see the old church torn down because the windows and doors were gone and it had become a haven for tramps who wanted to find shelter during the winter months. Tramps came to our door and asked for a breakfast handout and we knew they had spent the cold night in the old church. They never harmed us but sometimes they did frighten mother and I.

Joe Mac's wife owned a farm north of Republic that had grape vineyards on it. Daddy worked for her in the late winter and spring. In the summer and fall he worked in the R. A. Beale apple orchards.

UNCLE JOHN

When I was a sophomore in high school my Uncle John and his family decided to come to Missouri from Oklahoma. They came during the month of August and had a crate of watermelons shipped to us by railroad which we all enjoyed very much. Our house was too small for an extra family of six, three teenage girls and one boy ten years old. We could handle the food problems but not the sleeping problems. Several of us had to sleep on the floor. It is the only time I remember my father being in or taking anyone to the local saloon for beer. Uncle John loved to read Zane Grey books. He found "When a Man's a Man" and spent several hours sitting on the ground in the front yard reading it. One daughter did not enjoy herself. She was in love with a young man back home and she could not think of anything else or take an interest in our life. She married him soon after they returned and they are still alive and living in Oklahoma. I had a problem trying to entertain youngsters whom I did not know very well but we got along. Uncle John wanted to see Missouri and he seemed to like it but all he could talk about were the trees. He lived in a prairie state. He wanted to go to Arkansas but he never got there.

GOING BACK TO OKLAHOMA

Uncle Worth died in Beaver, Oklahoma. He had moved his cobbler shop from Jet to Beaver because he wanted to be near his niece, Althea Halstead Thomas (my cousin) and her husband Shirley Thomas and family who had moved from Jet to Knowles, Oklahoma. I had the privilege of visiting and seeing the buildings and life in a small western frontier town with its false stone fronts and board sidewalks. Beaver is a ghost town today.

But the story of going to Knowles and Beaver is an unusual one and a good picture of my father's thoughts and reactions. My father was not notified of Uncle Worth's death in time because it came so suddenly. He was given two days to go. He decided he should take me along because I was a blood relative and that mother should stay home, look after the place, and tend the garden while we were gone, much to her disgust.

The first thing to consider was how to get there. Daddy knew that there was a train to Knowles but he had heard that there was bus line. He thought that he could get there more quickly so we went by railroad to Jet, Oklahoma, and there was a bus from Jet to Woodward. We traveled as fast as we could but daddy did not stop to inquire about a bus out of Woodward to Knowles. We tried to tell him to inquire but he was so sure he had heard about a bus that he would not listen.

In August it can be unbearable to travel in northwestern Oklahoma. We were fortunate to get into the small western town of Woodward about 7 o'clock at night by bus and we learned the bus did not go any further. We started to walk to the railway station where we were soon told that the station had closed at 6 P.M. and would not open until 8 the next morning and that there was no passenger trains until after noon. We knew that the funeral was set for 11 o'clock the next morning and there was no way of notifying Shirley as to where we were – no telephone service. We did find a small lodging house but the lady had only one room with a double bed. Daddy had to tell her that we were father and daughter. By paying her extra money she managed to put a small cot in the room for me. I was tired, frightened, and hot but I managed to comfort my father. When we got in the room he sat down and sobbed his heart out. I never felt more sorry for him than I did that evening, but I think that if he had listened and understood that he was in a world of open country and no conveniences he would have found a better way. He slept little on that hot night but I was so tired and worried that I fell asleep almost immediately.

The next morning our landlady gave us our breakfast. We had not eaten since noon the day before. We were at the railroad station as soon as it opened and sent a wire to Shirley that we had gotten that far and that was it. Shirley answered our wire in about an hour stating that he would delay the funeral until we could get there. He drove his old Ford eighty miles to rescue us. He came as fast as the old Ford would bring him and we walked into the church about 3 o'clock that afternoon. The funeral started immediately. There was no embalming in those days and the climate was so hot that a body could not be kept very long. We accompanied the body to a small cemetery on a high ridge in the plains.

I had the privilege of going back to that cemetery and finding Uncle Worth's grave after the dust bowl era. During the dust bowl that cemetery was completely covered with two or three feet of dust. When I went back, the dust bowl debris had been cleared away and the grave sites were in good condition. In 1990, my cousin, Uncle John's son, went out and replaced the marker with a nice tombstone. I should have done it myself or else moved the body to be near other members of the family. Uncle Worth was a loner and his body lies buried more than two hundred miles from any relatives.

One more description of that wild ride is the wheat fields. We did drive by Old Fort Supply which was an army station and kept in fairly good condition. Shirley mentioned it and I would have liked to see the famous old land mark but we could not take the time. I will never forget the wheat fields. Wheat had risen to a dollar a bushel and every farmer wanted to make a fortune. The wheat was ripe and ready to be harvested. The road was dirt but considered a highway. There were no fences or buildings along this highway just golden ripe wheat blowing in the wind. When a breeze hit it, a wave like the ocean was formed and as you looked at the waves you felt like you were on an ocean liner that was rocking. I was fascinated but I grew dizzy, I could hardly sit up. I do not know how Shirley managed to drive his car.

As for my father I think he learned a lesson not to be so hasty and stubborn and to take time to study a situation. Poor Shirley was ill after that wild ride and did not live very long. The family moved back to Jet.

AUNT STELLA

When I was a senior in high school we were notified that my Aunt Stella, who was my father's oldest sister and the oldest child in the Crain family, had become very ill. It was about Christmas time and I could leave school. Much to mother's delight we three could go. I do not think daddy wanted to but he loved his sister despite all their spats about her first husband.

Estell or Stella as we call her had been married three times. The first time in Indiana to J. W. Burnham, who caused most of the trouble between Aunt Stella and daddy. To this union were born two children, Robert or Bob, who lived in Jet and a daughter, Polly, who died in early childhood. When the Cherokee Strip opened Stella's family had settled with her parents and brother, Worth, on a homestead near ours. There her husband died. He drank and caroused around in later life. Once my father chased him around the house with a gun and threatened to kill him for mistreating his sister until my grandfather separated them. After his death, she married Eugene Halstead of Wellington, Kansas. She had know him in Kansas. Eugene was a good friend of daddy's. After the Cherokee Strip opened he had followed and lived not far from us. This couple had two children, Altha, who later married Shirley Thomas, and Elegin who later operated the first telephone exchange in Goltry. This marriage did not work out. Estella worked at the Goltry exchange and also operated a hotel in Jet. There she met and married a well—known doctor. Later this couple moved to Enid where Dr. Fraser operated a private hospital in his own home for cancer victims. Aunt Stella nursed his patients.

Dr. Fraser felt that he had discovered a cure for cancer but he would not reveal it. He was an able and learned man and my father like him. He did tell us a little about his method but after a few months following Aunt Stella's death he died without revealing his secret. His method did not cure all his patients. Aunt Stella was a brown—haired, brown—eyed beauty who was always so proud of her appearance. So proud that when she grew older and stout she did what many women of her time did. She wanted to keep a perfect 24 inch waist line and so she laced her corsets so tight she eventually overlapped one rib. The irritation caused cancer to develop. She tried to keep it from the doctor until the cancer was too far developed and nothing could be done.

When we arrived in Enid she was too ill to see us but we were treated kindly by the doctor and her daughter Altha Thomas who was in charge of the household. That first night in the home we were given beds on one of the balconies of the house. Since it was December and very cold in Enid we were kept comfortable by portable gas heaters. (By this date Enid was one of the big oil and gas distributors in the nation.) I had never been in a home where natural gas was used for heat and cooking. I was fascinated, awed, and amazed by the glow from the heater. It is almost the only memory I have of that visit.

The next morning my Aunt was better and she called my mother and I to come to her room. She had Altha take a large glass plate out of her buffet and she presented it to me because I was a Crain heir. It was an heirloom, a clear glass cake plate with the Three Graces outlined on the bottom. She said it had belonged to her mother and since my grandmother had died before my father was married she wanted me to have it. The plate must have been carried by covered wagon from Indiana to Kansas to Oklahoma. I was shy but I tried to thank her as best I could. She died that night and since it was bad weather we decided not to stay for the funeral. My father did not say much about the plate but I know he was pleased. She never liked my mother. She might have resented her because she thought that my father would never marry and when he died would leave part of his homestead and property to his brothers and sisters. However he did marry and all hope of that was gone. My parents and relatives said that Aunt Stella had all my grandparent's possessions and I was the only one in the family she remembered. I do not know why unless I was the heir to the whole family since Aunt Stella was the oldest child, my father was next oldest and I was his only child. Many years afterwards I was supposed to have received all the valuable papers of the

Crain family from her but no one else received anything. Even Altha's daughter thought I had them. My father always said that Altha got everything but where did it go?

MY FRIEND MARTHA AND OTHER STORIES

While I was a senior in high school my friend, Martha, and I remained comrades. Martha graduated from Republic High School the year before me. Her family had moved seven times since I mentioned her last. She was a good student and since her family was very poor she applied for a teaching job in our local fourth grade. In those days one could graduate from high school, pass the county board exams, go to summer school at Springfield State Teachers' College one summer session and teach in the grade school next term as Martha did. She was a good teacher and when our school day was over, she would come by my house and I would walk almost home with her, (about a mile), then I would return. That was the only exercise I got that year as I was carrying five basic courses and a correspondence course in second year Spanish.

Martha and I had all kinds of girl problems and stories to tell each other on those walks. Daddy always seemed to enjoy those days and was nice to Martha although he teased her too much. Mother liked Martha and often invited her to stay for supper which she enjoyed. Those walks were the highlight of my senior year. Mother got supper and she and daddy would be ready to eat when I returned. How daddy let me out of the house for a walk I will never know.

When I was a junior I became discouraged with my school work and wanted to quit. I felt that I did not receive recognition from my Spanish teacher and that he was always praising a friend more than me. I had never had to take second place and it hurt. Also my superintendent was friendly with the Home Economics teacher who was a socialite and could not see me. I hated cooking, was shy and a bookworm so I got C's in cooking class. I came home one night and cried and said that I did not want to go to school. At first my father didn't say much although he knew I was very unhappy. Finally he said, "You don't have to go to school unless you want to. You can stay home and help your mother." I looked at him with surprise and thought if I do not have to go I will try again. I did and things were a little easier.

After several months my father was working in the apple orchard and he found out that one of his fellow workers had paid the Spanish teacher a fairly large sum of money to raise his daughter's grades and praise her over me. In the meantime though I had my courage back and was happy and working again.

But I did not like cooking until after I had finished college and stayed in a home in Michigan where I was teaching.

In the spring when I was a senior I began to "feel my oats". One morning at the breakfast table we were talking about U.S. History books and I had either read or got the idea some place that the authors of history books expressed their own Republican or Democratic ideas so I started "shouting my big mouth off" about the fact that the authors were Republican and wrote their data with a Republican attitude. I noticed that daddy suddenly became quiet and listened. He became angry and said, "Those writers are national and international authors and they are renowned writers. They would never let politics enter into their writings. Don't you ever dare to question what a renowned writer would say. It's not right to question your superiors." He got up from the table and left the house and there I sat feeling like a whipped puppy. Mother aid, "You better keep still. You know he would never let you question your superiors." Everything was quiet around our house the rest of the day. I kept quiet but it took me down a peg or two.

HIGH SCHOOL GRADUATION

About a month before school closed, I came home from school with my head in the clouds. My principal had informed me that I was to be the Valedictorian and that I had my choice of the college scholarships offered. At the table daddy looked at me and said, "Joe McMillan next door asked me this morning if I knew what my daughter was achieving in school and I told him that I didn't know."

Joe said, "Your daughter had the highest average."

Joe was a member of the school board so he knew before we did.

My father was proud of me but he just could not understand that I wanted to have a class ring to wear and that I would need some fancy graduation dresses to wear to the activities. Fortunately my mother had worked the summer before at the Fuhr Tomato Canning Factory and saved enough money to pay for my ring and buy the materials to make my dresses (we did not wear caps and gowns). She spent hours sewing for me and beading two of my dresses (crepe de chine).

Daddy was proud of me but that pride did not change his ideas that a woman liked to have new clothes and look pretty. He was always that way. He always had a good suit but he could not understand that we women could not wear the same dress and hat year after year. Why he felt that way I do not know. He never seemed to notice people's clothes. My parents attended all my graduation activities with pride and bragged about my achievements.

COLLEGE

Soon after graduation from high school a shoe factory opened in Republic. This factory took young inexperienced workers at the rate of about $1.30 a day for a training period. I knew I had to work for money for college and I started there. I hated my job. I sewed the uppers for men's and boy's shoes. I hated using the leather sewing machine but I had to earn as much as I could. My family did not want me to do it but they understood and my father began to worry about how he was going to finance my scholarship. I worked all summer without rest or vacation. The work was not hard but tedious and I was not accustomed to having a foreman stand over me.

When the day of registration came my family rose early and we took the bus into Springfield and the street car to South West Missouri State Teachers' College.

My father did not want me to go. He said that he did not think I was physically able but he did not forbid me. He and mother went with me. His reason was that he could not see where the money was coming from.

I had no trouble registering and then went to the dean's office for a list of places where I might work for my room and board. We selected the best possible one. It was about a mile from the college down South National Avenue on Meadowmere. Daddy said he did not like walking but my mother said that she would go with me. She did and I walked back with her to the college where she and daddy took the street car and bus back to Republic.

The place I found was the home of a Russian Jewish family with two children, a four year old boy and a seven year old girl. The little boy was called Jerome. His father had an antique shop and traveled around southwest Missouri. He would be gone for two weeks at a time. The girl went to grade school and came home with head lice much to my horror because I had to sleep with her. The mother, born in Russia, was the most beautiful woman I have ever seen. She was a hostess in a bar at night.

I knew nothing about the food habits of Russian Jews and little about their way of life. I must have been a curiosity to them too. It was a five room house and I had no room of my own but shared a room with the children. The mother left the home every day about one o'clock and came home at one in the morning. My duties were to get the children up in the morning, get the girl started to school, then come home at 4 in the afternoon, find Jerome playing in the neighborhood, get their evening meal, and put them to bed about nine. Then I could study. This was all a strange experience for me but I managed to do what was expected. The lady of the house was young, knew nothing about housework and did not relate to her family. Her marriage had been an arrangement between the parents. She and I got along well because I taught her about sewing, laundry, and cleaning but I had to learn cooking from her and it was Russian style.

LEARNING INDEPENDENCE

Meanwhile my father realized that I was determined to go to college even to work my way through. About this time there was a land boom in the Florida Everglades. He had a friend and they had left their homesteads in Oklahoma back in 1907 and taken a vacation trip to Florida. There he bought 20 acres of land in the Everglades. It was undeveloped but he had kept the taxes paid. He decided to sell the land and use the money to put me through college. He sold the land to a man named Martin Howard in Republic. Martin Howard was the Green County clerk and went back and forth each day on the train to work at the county court house in Springfield. My father sold this land to Martin for three thousand dollars and I received a B.S. in Education Degree from it.

I stayed with the Russian Jewish family until March of 1925. In one of my classes in education was a lady of 40 years whose husband was ill and could not work. She needed money to live and go to college so she rented out her dining room to me and another female student whom I did not know. She put another bed in it and fixed up a section of her basement for us for light housekeeping rooms. I lived there for more than a year. Things were really much easier and I had to walk only a half block to classes. Then the family moved away and I found another light housekeeping room about two blocks away. I enjoyed living in this home and going to college.

As soon as daddy had the money he put a certain amount in the bank in my name and I had to learn how to apportion it and pay my expenses with personal checks. I will always honor my father for teaching me how to handle money to pay my expense and how to save. I did not go home every weekend but stayed and used the library for my lesson assignments.

In 1925 my parents came to Springfield, rented a room on South Street and took me to the Rebecca Lodge on Commercial Street and saw that I was initiated into the order. I did not want to go and had refused several times because I was not interested. They loved the Order from their early life in Oklahoma and determined that I must be a Rebecca. I was trapped and went with them to be initiated. After the initiation I joined the Order for keeps. I am still a member and have been since 1925, even transferring to Michigan. When I came to Fowlerville, I served as Noble Grand in the Fowlerville Lodge and when that lodge was abandoned I joined the Perry Lodge. I am glad now that they insisted as I feel very comfortable and happy in the Order.

The next year I moved to another boarding place about two blocks away and lived there almost three years. The lady's husband died and she had to sell the place and leave Springfield. I was happy in this house and made some new friends. I learned about developing a life of my own and being independent.

During the winter of 1927–28 I became ill and had to stay at home. While we had lived at the brick house in Republic I had a bout of malaria and was very ill. Malaria is a recurrent disease and I mixed a little overwork with it. Then in the spring I returned to college and of course had to go during the hot summer session to make up for the lost term.

SCHOOL TEACHER

I began to think about a job. School teaching in those days was about the only kind of work a girl could find. With the help of my school placement agency I applied for a high school teaching job at Brandsville, Missouri. Brandsville is about 80 miles from Springfield on the Memphis Branch of the Frisco Railroad. I took the railroad train one hot Saturday in July to apply. Brandsville was the Georgia Peach shipping point on the Frisco in the Ozark Hills on the Missouri–Arkansas Line, in the rugged and picturesque big spring section of the state.

The school was a newly created three teacher high school in a village with two general stores, a post office, a blacksmith shop, a barber shop, a restaurant, a railroad station with daily passenger service, a club house, and several homes. I had never been in that part of the Ozarks before and I loved it. I got the job at one hundred dollars a month for nine months. I was qualified to teach Latin, all the social studies including American and European History, high school geography, American Government, Sociology, and Economics. I was elated when I got back to Springfield that Saturday night. Because I could not go home for another week my first task was to write a letter informing my parents of my good luck.

My parents came for my graduation and we took my belongings home on the train two days after graduation. My father used common sense and bought me a large wardrobe trunk for my graduation gift. Mother had much to do with it for I had only a small suitcase to carry my clothes and some food from Republic to Springfield and back. The other thing I needed was a watch and I had to buy that myself out of college expenses. I used that watch until some time in the late nineteen–fifties. I also bought my graduation picture and pin. My expenses for a four year B.S. in Education was 2,950 dollars.

I spent the summer of 1928 at home in Republic sewing. I had to have clothes for my new job and in those days one had to make clothes as it was difficult to buy them. My mother helped me. My father made me a large wooden box with metal handles on it to pack my books and teaching materials in so I was well prepared to begin my career. The metal box is in my shed here in Fowlerville and I treasure it very much.

BRANDSVILLE

In August of 1928 I went by train to Brandsville for my first year of work in a three teacher high school. The new teachers were all members of the summer 1928 session of Southwest Missouri State Teachers' College in Springfield. The superintendent was Ed Kizer whom I knew by sight and the other lady was Ruth Toalson whom I had had English classes with. Ruth and I decided to room together and we found a one room apartment with the Rose Sisters in a house south of the high school. It was a make–shift room but we were happy to find that.

We had a double bed, a dresser, a small table, a topsy wood burning heat stove, a three burner kerosene cook stove, a shelf for dishes, two clothes racks and two chairs, and room for our trunks. We could have our breakfast in our room, lunch with the Ball sisters, and our evening meal at a small restaurant by the Post Office which had just opened. The reason for the restaurant's opening was the reopening of an old iron ore smelter about five miles out of town. Laura Ball who was about 24 years of age was the school secretary so we felt we were safe and protected there. In those days teachers were restricted if they were females. They were not allowed a social life. No husbands or boyfriends and no smoking or drinking. No partying at all.

There were two groups in the town, a religious one and a social one. The religious group was always on guard and we had to watch everything we did or said to the students. There was one small country church about a mile west of town but no minister and an evening service about every two months. The social group occasionally held dances on Saturday nights at the Community House to which we were invited but we steered clear of them too. When important town meetings were held we had to attend them. The people were friendly and we had pleasant times with them in their homes. We always had to watch what we said or did in school and out.

I was very happy there. If you were a freshman and only sophomore subjects were offered that year you had to take sophomore subjects, freshman subjects the next year. If you were a junior and senior subjects were offered you had to take senior subjects. It may sound unreasonable but it worked and that year we graduated a class of fourteen, five of whom took the rural teacher's exams in June, went to summer school at Teachers' College and taught rural schools the following winter. Five of those seniors were successful enough to go on to the University and become college teachers and professors in twenty years time.

I loved my new job in the hill country. The school house was located in a grove of hickory nut trees and when I wanted a little snack I could sit on a log in the school yard and crack hickory nuts. There was no stream near the town but there were sink holes, caves, wild plants, wild flowers, and trees.

It was a never–ending treat to leave school at 4 o'clock and go with Ruth and Laura for a long hike down the railroad tracks or the highway for 2 or 3 miles. We had to avoid the woods because of rattlesnakes and ticks but we had fun. Early in the year we realized that our students had no form of recreation. Weekends, especially Saturday afternoon and Sundays, we would get a group of them to bring a brown bag lunch and we would take a five mile hike to some interesting spot. In the spring we hired a truck with side boards and visited some of the big springs in the region, places some of the natives had not seen. Our pupils seemed to live for these weekend excursions. We did not have any discipline problems in school either because these hillbilly kids had respect and love for us and they worked in school. They had no hope in life and their parents sent them to high school with the idea that this was their chance to better their condition. They had enough sense to take advantage of the opportunity. We did have light snows in the winter that lasted a day or two and at Christmas time I caught a cold which became an abscess in one lung. I went home and had to miss school for two weeks.

AN UNHAPPY TIME

The next year Ruth and I were rehired. Ruth as superintendent and I as principal. I was having too good a time and drifting away from my father and his teachings. So in August of 1929 he decided to leave the house in Republic and rent rooms at Brandsville so I could be at home and teach too. Ruth rented a room in a house near the school and we got a nice three room apartment in back of the restaurant. I had to go along with my father's plans and he and mother fixed up the apartment. Mother did not say much but she did her part. When school started I was not free as before. I was expected to leave school at 4 o'clock and go home to my family in the apartment. I could not be myself and mingle with friends as before. The people of Brandsville were friendly to my folks but the situation was different and difficult.

Daddy made a bargain with a farmer about a mile east of Brandsville to cut down the small trees on his land and split them into firewood and he spent his mornings walking to the place and returning in the afternoons after his day's work. Some days he could not work because of rain so he got acquainted with some of the older men around town at the blacksmith shop down the street from our apartment. Men liked to gather there each day to discuss the weather, politics, local affairs, etc. He heard all the things that had happened in the town.

When we had local basketball games at night I had to attend and sometimes sell tickets at the door. Daddy could not understand why basketball was such an important event in that little town and community and why I had to go. Mother went with me each time and he would be crabby. He did not care for sports and he just could not understand why anyone else did. I was handicapped. I could not be friends and go for walks with my students at all.

I had had a seventeen year old boy in my Latin class the first year whom I will call Jim who had developed a crush on me. I knew it and all the school and town knew it. All I could do was overlook it and treat him as I would any of my pupils. He was seventeen and I was twenty–six years old. The second year I was there his parents, who lived in another town, decided to put him in the West Plains School system. He hated it and on weekends he would run away from home, come to Brandsville and sometimes to the apartment to see me. Of course daddy heard the whole story and he thought Jim was a crazy kid and would never amount to anything. All I could do was visit with Jim and be nice to him. Then my parents began to think Ruth was too bossy and they did not like her.

About the last February daddy began to get homesick and being an old farmer he thought he should go home and plant a garden. He became crabby with both mother and me and mother said to me, "I guess I had better go home with him and you can have a little peace the rest of the year."

I could not stay in the three room apartment alone and daddy talked to one of his new friends at the blacksmith shop and got a room for me in his home. He was one of the school board members, Uncle Phin McMillan, and I was conscious of the fact that I could not do anything for three whole months without being under strict surveillance. I liked the McMillans, they were good people. They had no children and lived in a three room house. They gave me their bedroom and cared for me as if I had been their own. She was an excellent cook so I faired well and lost some of my tenseness. Daddy did me a favor but he did not know it. As a result I did not want to teach in Brandsville another year, and Ruth decided to move too. We did try to resume the hikes with the students. It was with regret that I left my students in that school and the whole community hated to see me go.

As soon as school was out I came home. Daddy was in good spirits but I had joined the Yates–Fisher Teachers' Agency in Chicago and was offered a school at Atlanta, Michigan at double my old salary. I accepted without any hesitation.

After I came home I had a bad recurrence of malaria for a short time. The result of tension over my work and home life.

In July of that year I had a letter from my new superintendent in Atlanta that I had met the State Board's O.K. and if I could not get a certificate to teach in Michigan he would have to look for a new principal. I was scared. I went to President Roy Ellis at Teachers' College and explained my situation and received wonderful support. President Ellis notified the State Board that I was a graduate of a college belonging to the North Central Association of Colleges and Universities. I spent two weeks "sweating blood" because I needed a job and it was getting too late in the season. I remember sitting on the cistern top at home in Republic wondering why I did not hear from the State Board of Michigan. My father kept out of the picture but he went to the Post Office every morning to get the mail. He did not talk much but I knew he was worried. About the middle of August I received two letters, one from the State Board with a Life Certificate to teach in the State of Michigan and one from Atlanta telling me when to come to my new position. I was relieved. I had to wait for the State Board to meet to issue my certificate and they had chosen not to meet until the middle of the month. I received a Life Certificate to teach in the State of Michigan by sending in my credentials and paying a fee of two dollars. I had two weeks to prepare for my long trip to Michigan. My father helped me in every way he could, going with me to the railway station to buy my ticket which was a new experience for my agent as he had never sold a ticket so far away. He worked on that ticket. I did not have any trouble. I had done very well and I learned a lot. I had never been east of the Mississippi River and knew nothing about Detroit or northern Michigan.

MICHIGAN

When I boarded the train in Republic for Michigan in August 1930, an inner feeling came to me that I would never come back to Missouri to live. I do not know why but it was a deep emotional feeling. I have gone back for summers and Christmas vacations but not to live and now I do not think I ever will.

My trip on the train was a long one, two days and three nights, full of strange new sights, big cities, a different country side and great forests.

I remember most vividly waking up the second morning and looking out the car window to see morning fog and miles of pine forests (near Oscoda), no buildings just trees. I thought I must be in Alaska.

When I got off the train in Gaylord at about 8:30 in the morning I went across the street to a cafe for breakfast. The dining room was open with tables beautifully set with table linens and flowers but no one answered the doorbell. I went back to the depot where the agent told me I was too early. No one was up at that hour of the morning.

When I received a letter from home, my father had worried about me, a young woman alone on a trip to an unknown land. He was frightened and wished he had gone with me. I was safe however, in a world unknown to me. I adjusted although I was a curiosity to the northern people because of my southern accent and language. I did not have a Christmas at home for five years because I could not make the trip in time. However I enjoyed a different Christmas with Northerners. I had had malaria and was still very weak so I did as my hometown doctor told me, "Go north and freeze it out of you." I would teach school all day long, go to the hotel at 4 o'clock, go to bed for some rest until supper time, eat and go back to bed and then begin a new day. I did that until Christmas and I have not had an attack of malaria since. It was the beginning of a whole new life for my parents too and they learned to survive.

In 1935 Daddy sold our Oklahoma homestead to Mr. Clark from Goltry for a very good price accepting a mortgage on it. He thought he would have enough money to pay his and mother's way for the rest of their life but he did not count on inflation. He placed his money in the Jet Bank and transferred it to Republic as he needed it. Soon after that someone killed the Jet banker and robbed the bank. A moratorium was declared on the bank for several years and I had to help daddy. It worked out and the Jet Bank recovered its finances.

MEXICO CITY

In 1937 summer tours became the thing and I joined one to Mexico City to go to the National University of Mexico. Daddy wanted me to go but he said that Mexico was a foreign country and he did not trust Mexicans. All went well for me. I wrote a letter every day to my parents but I did not hear from them. After I had been at the University for more than three weeks I went down to the dining room of the hotel and someone in my group came and told me that there was a telegram for me posted on the cashier's window. Hurriedly I went to get it and was told that my parents had had no word from me since I left Missouri. My tour guide took me on the street car to a telegraph station in downtown Mexico City. I was frightened but with my guide's help the station sent a telegram to Republic that I was alive and doing well and had written to them every day. It seems that daddy worried, went to the post office every morning but no letter. Finally he reached the point where he went to the railway station, gave the address I had left as to where I could be found and sent the message. Mr. Haymes, the agent, sent the message to Mexico City saying he had never sent a telegram outside the nation but he would try. He tried and they waited several hours for an answer. Daddy almost "sweat blood." He was sure some bandit had killed us. (That was in the days of Pancho

Villa's raids in Mexico.) He walked the streets and the agent was upset too. Mother remained quiet. They waited two days and finally got an answer from me. Two weeks after that they received all my letters in one big packet and calmed down. There was an airline strike and no planes had gone out of Mexico until the strike was over. Since we had no other way except air mail I did not know what was happening in Missouri or Mexico. When I came home in the middle of August all was calm and peaceful but that was one of the worst times in my father's life.

BLINDNESS

In 1938 daddy began to go blind. He went to an eye specialist and learned that he had cataracts. In our town was an elderly man who had had an operation for cataracts and it was not very successful since doctors were just learning how to treat them. Father finally went to a doctor to talk about an operation and the doctor told him he could operate when his eyes were ready but the operation would cost over a thousand dollars. A thousand dollars was a big sum in those days and daddy said he would not pay it. He was scared to death of a hospital. He would not go to one to see his relatives because he was so afraid of them. The result was that he did not do anything and so he was ten years going blind. It was not so bad for me since I was not home but it was a hard life for my mother who had to live with him.

In those days there was no Social Security. Old folks in Missouri organized clubs in which they gave dimes each month and formed an organization thinking they could become a strong national group and get help in that way but the whole thing fell through. My father began to lose faith in everything. One year he failed to vote in the school election for a millage proposal. He came home and said he had voted to get schooling for his daughter and other people could do the same for their children. I was dismayed because he had never had that attitude before, had always been a conscientious voter, a socialist in the early days but when World War I occurred and the socialist refused to fight because of their religious beliefs he became a Democrat and remained one the rest of his life. He served on the city election board so I became acquainted with politics early in life and had to vote to please him.

In 1939 while I was home for the summer daddy began to talk about coming to Michigan just to see the country. He was curious so I decided to have him come before school started. We decided to do it while he could still see the world around him. Mother wanted to come too but he thought she should stay and take care of the garden and place. She was disappointed as usual.

They were having hot humid weather in Missouri and the temperature was in the nineties. I suggested that he put his jacket and sweater in his suitcase but he did not think he would need them. I persuaded him that he was leaving hot Missouri for the north country. I laughed at him because before we got to St. Louis on the train he had to have his jacket out of his suitcase. He enjoyed the trip and had to visit with others on the train and bus. He was especially interested in the crops growing along the railway tracks more than the famous railway station in St. Louis or the big city of Detroit. What interested him the most were the big potato fields around Gaylord. He could not understand why they were so different from those in Missouri, all vines and few potatoes.

I took him to see the school in Atlanta, Michigan, where I taught and the huge log community house in Atlanta built by W.P.A. and to visit my friends. He enjoyed his trip but I could not trust him to go home alone because of his growing blindness. I took him as far as St. Louis. When he boarded the train in St. Louis I put him in the protection of the conductor who guided him to Springfield. I worried until I knew he was safely back in Republic. He was happy to return home.

A year later he became the janitor at the Christian Church just three doors down the street from our home. Mother helped and he enjoyed the work. We had been members of the church since 1917. In the winter he would go early and start the coal fire in the big stove at the back of the room. Then a half hour before church time he would go back and ring the big bell in the belfry, go home, change his clothes and come back for the service.

One Sunday morning in March he rang the bell and stopped to stoke up the coal in the stove. For some reason the stove shot out a blast of smoke and he was covered with soot. At that moment in came one of the young women. Looking at him covered with soot she made some remarks to her girlfriends and teased him. It made him angry. He came home, sent someone to finish his chores at the church and never entered the church gain. Once in a while he would go to the Methodist Church on Sunday. He did not turn against churches but read his Bible at home as long as he could see.

JIM

A short time after we had returned from Brandsville and I had gone to teach school in Michigan, my Brandsville student, Jim Miller, graduated from high school and taught a rural school for a time. Because he had relatives in Springfield he spent his summers with them and attended Southwest Missouri State Teachers' College to work on his Bachelor's Degree. He came several times and we had a good visit. The reader will remember that daddy did not like Jim at Brandsville. He thought he was just a kid and would not amount to anything but was nice to him and mother went out of her way to cook some good meals.

After that, World War II broke out. Jim's mother and father died and he moved to Kansas to spend his life with his older sister. There he taught school, went to Kansas State Teachers' College and grew up. When war broke out he was drafted and I went to Kansas one summer to visit his home. He gave me two books of poetry that he had written to keep and have published for him. I failed him because I did not know how to get poetry published. We corresponded while he was in France and Belgium. He was caught in the Battle of the Bulge but escaped unharmed. When the war was over he came home to Kansas and since I was home from Big Rapids, Michigan, I agreed to go to Kansas to see him. It was a great event in his life to be able to come home from the war and know that I would come to Kansas. He had been home a day and a half when I came.

I had come to Republic for Christmas and now I was leaving home to go to see Jim in Kansas. My father could not understand my leaving when I had only two weeks at home. He did not say much but he went with me to the bus station.

Jim, his family and I had a happy time in Kansas. I stayed two days and came back to Missouri. Father did not meet me at the bus station and when I got home he stared and kept silent. I knew I was in the dog house but I tried to be my usual self and mother was her usual self. Late that night he said to me, "If you have anything to tell me, I am willing to listen." He thought I had gone to Kansas and married Jim. Mother had tried to explain to him that I had gone out of friendship but he could not accept that. He was so sure that he had lost me. I should have done differently but could not say much. There was not much I could say and I did not see what I had done wrong. I had to go back to Michigan the next day. I came back with a lump in my throat. Mother said that he did not get over his fright for some time but he never seemed the same. He was so sure that I had planned to marry Jim and that I had not told him. We never mentioned the affair again.

Jim taught the next two years at Culver-stockton College in Missouri, then went on to teach in a Negro college for boys near Cairo, Illinois, where he distinguished himself as a counselor to the boys. He retired and died in Kansas about four years later. His body was brought back to Bakersfield, Missouri, for burial not far from Brandsville.

DEPRESSION YEARS

The Depression Years came. Franklin Roosevelt became President of the United States. Daddy liked President Roosevelt and listened to his fireside chats on the radio. About that time some congressmen introduced a bill that if a farmer in the midwest had sold his land and accepted a mortgage as payment he could not force the payment of that mortgage. The bill was passed to help struggling young farmers but with no thought of the families depending on the mortgage for their sustenance. Daddy had accepted a mortgage when he sold his homestead and he began to worry because that was all he had left to live on. He watched all the articles in the Springfield Leader for news and he nearly lost his mind.

Summer came and I had returned home from teaching in Michigan. As blind as he was he would walk down the street to the drug store and buy the paper for news. When he brought the paper home I had to sit down and read it for news about the bill. He was so worried that I thought he was going to go berserk. Rumors were that President Roosevelt did not favor the bill and finally vetoed it. Congress could not override his veto so daddy's problems were solved. The mortgage was paid and daddy had his money in the bank. He was happy. He thought he would have enough money to keep him and mother for the rest of their lives.

In 1941 came the bank holiday. I was back in Michigan and had only eight cents in my purse. I could not spend that because I had to have postage to write home. My father had eight dollars in the Republic Bank. I was fortunate. In Atlanta the owner of the general store, Mike Doty, kept most of his money in a safe in the store and the next Friday our teachers' checks were due. Out of the kindness of his heart Mike Doty took the money from his own safe to the school board to pay the teachers' salary until the bank could open. The bank holiday lasted two weeks and we did not know what would happen after that. I sent money in a letter to my parents which was a risky thing to do. I asked my hotel owner what to do. He said, "I am in trouble too. I have to depend on the local grocer and buy my food supplies on time so I will carry all of you (my roomers and boarders) on time. There is nothing any of us can do until this crisis is over."

In Atlanta, Michigan, we were fortunate. When the bank holiday ended our little private bank opened and paid a hundred per cent on the dollar. Rumors had circulated for years that the little bank was about to fail but after that there were no more rumors and the private bank has grown into a powerful one today.

In Republic, Missouri we were not so fortunate. The bank never opened its doors again for business. I lost a thousand dollars in savings. Many older people in the community lost their life savings and almost starved to death until they could go on welfare. My father was fortunate. He had kept his money in the Jet, Oklahoma bank and checked out a little bit at a time as he needed it. The Jet Bank was safe too. We both put our money in the Bank of Billings and used that bank for many years. Billings was the first town west, about seven miles from Republic. A thousand dollars does not seem like much today but in those days it was a fortune. I survived the loss.

Daddy's blindness increased and when I was home in the summer and he had to transact business I had to go with him. I learned to be eyes and ears for him.

He thought when he sold the homestead he would have enough to keep his family for the rest of his life but he just lived too long and about a year before he died he was out of money and that nearly killed him. He and mother had to go on welfare and because I was a teacher not at home and in a different state I had to support them. At that time Missouri was beginning its welfare program. They were certainly cheap for my mother and father each received six dollars a month.

Two days after my father's funeral the welfare person was there to tell me she had seen the notice of his death in the paper and that she had taken his name off her list. I was really angry but did not say very much except that while she was at it should take my mother's name off too. She wanted to know why and I simply said that she would no longer be living in the state. That was that. She had gone around town to the merchants and asked if my parents paid their bills with a check. One of the merchants told her to get out of his store for it was not any of her business.

I LOVE YOU

In March of 1947 my father began to worry about a garden. He was not able to see and he was too weak to go into the garden to work so he decided that mother was to do the gardening, that we must have a garden as usual. Mother said to him, "I am going to sit here on the davenport and let you feel my face and shoulders. I weigh a little over eighty pounds. I can't take care of you and work in a garden." He did as she directed and decided that that was out of the question.

Then he began to worry about the garden growing up to weeds so when I came in May I was sent into the garden. I did find some Swiss Chard that had come up voluntarily but it was too late for a garden. Once he wandered into the garden with his spade and tried to dig up the earth but he as doing more harm than good and I yelled at him to stop. He did but he walked into the wash house and sat down on a bench. He sat there for a long time and I could hear him sobbing so I went down and apologized for trying to tell him not to worry about the garden. I would take care of him and mother. He looked up at me and said something that I never heard him say before, "I love you and I feel that I am failing in my duty. I ought to be taking care of you but you know that I can't."

I spent about an hour trying to calm him
and telling him not to worry. I got him to cease
his sobbing and come with me to the house. I
had spent many hours with my father in the
past but that was the closest I ever felt to him.
We went to the house and never mentioned the
incident again.

When I came home from Big Rapids in June
1948, I found him worse than ever.

He had developed the habit of walking each
day for exercise along the fence from our front
gate to the back gate on the other street west of
us. His mind was not good and he would slip
out the back gate and go down the sidewalk
usually north to where my cousin Dolly lived
three blocks from home, then turn, walk east to
Main Street then turn and come back to the
front gate.

Mother and I had to watch him to see that
he did not get hurt but when we followed him
we never got close enough to him to let him
know we were following him. We never knew
when he would disappear and it was a constant
worry.

DEATH

In April of 1949 I received a letter from mother that told me father had had a stroke and was partially paralyzed but she could handle the situation until I got home. He had not been conscious of what he was doing at the breakfast table that morning. After eating he had said that he would walk in the yard. Mother had tried to clean up the house while he was in the yard. She was busy and suddenly heard a man's voice at the front door. A friend of ours had been walking down the street and saw him fall in the yard. When he got to him he was unconscious so he ran down the street to get some men to help him carry daddy to the house. The men brought daddy in unconscious and called Dr. Mitchell.

Daddy did come to and Dr. Mitchell said he was paralyzed but he could not say much more. For a time he could not talk or move so the men stayed with mother and helped her for a few hours. He was partly himself but he could not walk. He had to use a chair to push himself to the bathroom and mother had to help him. He would not leave the davenport and go to the bedroom to sleep, sat all night on the davenport and did not talk very much or show any interest in anything. Poor mother had some of her neighbors to help her until I got home the first of June.

When I came home he did not talk to me very much but I felt that he knew everything that was happening around him. He became cranky and we could not please him. He must have been going through some inner turmoil that we knew nothing about.

Mother and I moved their bed into the living room and got him to lie there. He wanted his small radio taken out of the room. It seemed to irritate him. We got him to use a small slop jar by sitting on an old cane bottom chair with the canning removed and the jar placed below. We could help him off and on the bed. People can improvise when they have to.

I wrote to my superintendent asking for a six week leave of absence beginning the first of September. I did not know what else to do. Dolly and her sister, Nellie, helped us all they could. By this time Aunt Minnie was an invalid. Most of mother's other sisters were dead.

One afternoon my mother and I were standing at the head of his bed anxiously looking down at his face. He was not breathing or so we thought and the perspiration was beginning to roll down his forehead. His night shirt was getting wetter and wetter. That morning he had talked with us when we fed him and mother had said that she had to go down to the washhouse and start a fire to boil the clothes, that she had to do some washing for him and us too. I helped carry the water from the hot water tank in the bathroom to fill up the boiler and we both carried water from the outside spigot in the yard to fill the washing machine and tubs for rinsing. These tasks daddy had always done for us.

"I think I can take care of the washing now but I want you to stay in the house and watch him and get him something if he wants it," she said.

I finished washing and drying our breakfast dishes and kept an eye on him then tried to straighten up the house, went to the washhouse a time or two, came back and heard him talking to himself. He kept looking at a picture on the wall and talking about it. I hardly understood what he was saying. He seemed to be mumbling to himself so I sat down on the davenport and listened. He was quiet for a minute and seemed to drift off to sleep. I moved around a little and he roused and began to talk. He did not know I was there. He began to speak a prayer which I had never heard before. I listened for a while and he quieted down and was sleeping, so I went out. Mother was hanging clothes on the line. She finished and started to empty the tubs of water. I came out of the kitchen and said to her, "Daddy has been saying a prayer but I don't understand what he was saying or what he meant. It doesn't make sense. I never heard him pray before except at mealtime." I repeated what I could remember of what he had said.

She looked at me rather queerly and I knew that she knew something I did not.

"I know what he was saying. He is delirious and wouldn't have repeated such words if he had been in his right mind. Do you remember when you were a little girl and we lived in

Oklahoma and always went to the Old Fellow's Lodge? He was chosen to be the Chaplain in the prayers for the meetings. At first he was worried because they had to be repeated word for word. He practiced at home and sometimes I had to listen and help him. Here he is repeating the Chaplain's prayer after fifty years. I just can't believe it. He really is sick and let's never tell or reveal what we have heard him say. As you know that is a secret organization and we are pledged never to reveal the secret work. He would be so chagrined if he knew what he had done. I was a Rebecca at the time and I knew and helped him, but I never let it go any farther. Let's keep it a secret as I know if he were aware of it he would never forgive himself."

In the afternoon he seemed to rouse and was his usual self until about four o'clock. He talked with us but could not eat much. Suddenly he grew quiet and went into a stupor. He did not seem to breathe and he began to sweat.

As mother and I were bending over him I wanted to call the doctor but mother said, "No, let's wait a bit. I have a feeling he will come out of it."

It was a warm day in July and mother and I watched him while constantly bathing his face. His bedclothes were wet with perspiration. He remained that way about thirty minutes. Suddenly the sweating stopped and we could feel a pulse. He opened his blind eyes and we could see recognition in his eyes. When we asked him how he felt he did not remember much but later he roused again and was rational.

We called Dr. Mitchell and when he came he said that was a part of the disease and that when the fluid came up and entered the heart that it would choke his heart but he could not say how long it would be. My cousins, Nellie and Dolly came. He lived three or four more days and appeared to be his usual self. In the afternoon he suddenly said, "I have to get up."

Mother said, "Are you sure?"

He had been up and sat in his makeshift toilet several times that day. He insisted so mother and I lifted him to the foot of the bed where he could slide into the chair. He did slide into the chair with us on each side. As he was sitting there I heard a peculiar breathing sound and then rattling in his throat and chest.

I said, "Mother, something is wrong. Let's get him back in the bed."

She made a supreme effort to lift him off the far side of the chair and I lifted him (170 pounds) on the bed. We pushed him back and raised his feet on the bed. He gasped and never breathed again.

Mother had wrenched her back and was almost screaming with pain but she stood there and I ran to the neighbors to call the doctor. He was busy and came just as soon as he could but father died while we were lifting him on to the bed. The doctor treated mother. She had to go to bed and stay while our relatives came after the undertaker had taken father.

CONCLUSION

Mother and I had made plans. I knew that she could never live at home alone and I had to go back to Big Rapids, Michigan, before school started.

One incident stands out in my memory very clearly. Mother and I had gone to the funeral home to view the body and express our views of how the funeral should be conducted. We were standing beside the coffin telling Uncle Bob Thermion that we were pleased with everything and how we wanted to proceed when suddenly mother had a coughing spell. Uncle Bob went to get her a glass of water and answer his telephone. When he walked out of the room she opened her purse and pulled out daddy's old–fashioned razor that his mother had given him fifty years before (the kind that had to be sharpened on a leather strap) and his gold watch (just the shell) that he had carried for many years and that had our pictures in the lid. She slipped them under his arm in the coffin. Uncle Bob came in and we finished our talk with him and left.

As we were walking home I expressed my surprise and mother said, "His mother gave him the razor when he was young and he carried and used it for some seventy–five years. I wasn't about to keep it. After all, what could we do with it. As for the watch, he carried it most of his adult life until watches were made with an open face. He had the works taken out and put in a new one that he could still put on a fob and carry in his pocket. I hope Uncle Bob never finds them for I have heard that sometimes undertakers check at the last moment to see if a favorite jewel has been slipped in."

We never knew whether the trick worked or not, but as mother had said they were daddy's most precious possessions and what would we do with them.

At the funeral service the Odd Fellow Lodge from Springfield put on an elaborate ceremony at the grave site. Some of the members were old friends of his. The year was 1949 and he had joined the young lodge at the old town of Jet in the Oklahoma Territory back in 1903 and had been an active member all those years.

We began to plan for selling the home and getting ready for a public auction. We were busy with so many tasks and mother was not well but the tasks were finished. I wonder how we did get through with them so well and so quickly. The preparation was good for taking our minds off our sorrow.

We did not sell the home but put it in the hands of our favorite attorney and he sold it for us two months after we came to Michigan. After the sale we spent the night with mother's sister, Minnie, who was alone.

There were seven big boxes shipped by express besides our three big trunks. We boarded the local train at Republic and the train took us safely through to Big Rapids, Michigan. We arrived the night before school was to open.

As we boarded the train and were going through Illinois I remember saying to my mother, "I want you to look forward to a new life in which you won't have the responsibility and troubles that you have had. I know it won't be easy but I know it is the only thing for us to do. You are about to collapse from the responsibility of caring for a blind man for ten years and doing it all alone since I couldn't be at home to help. You weigh about eighty pounds and look worn out. I want you to enjoy a new life which is certainly going to be different."

My mother looked at me and smiled, "I will try but sometimes I wonder if I will ever be able to get to Michigan alive."

She did and she lived ten years after that. I hope she was a little happier and relieved of her responsibilities. I think she was.

My father had lived eighty–nine years. A long life in those days. He had his faults, as we all do, but he had good qualities too. I never heard him use a vulgar word in my life. When I was born he made up his mind he had to live a decent life for his little girl. He did not drink and he never went out at night without my mother or me with him. He loved to stay home and work around the house. He was honest and sometimes exasperating but I will always respect his training and molding of my character to be honest and kind to others.

I end this tale with my mother sitting in the chair car of the train listening to the lonesome whistle of the old Wabash Cannonball as it wound its way along the Wabash River to its

destination in Detroit with the hope of beginning a new life.